ACRYLIC PORTRAIT PAINTING

ACRYLIC PORTRAIT PAINTING

BY HELEN VAN WYK

WATSON-GUPTILL PUBLICATIONS • NEW YORK

To Maximilian Aureal Rasko

First Published 1970 by Watson-Guptill Publications,
a division of Billboard Publications Inc., 165 West 46 Street,
New York, New York 10036
Manufactured in Japan.
All Rights Reserved.
No portion of the contents of this book may be reproduced
or used by any means without the written permission of
the publishers.
ISBN 0-8230-0075-3
Library of Congress Catalog Card Number: 70-125844

Contents

Demonstrations

Acknowledgments

I wish to thank M. Grumbacher, Inc., who manufacture Hyplar; Bocour Artist Colors, Inc., who manufacture Aqua-Tec; and Permanent Pigments, Inc., who manufacture Liquitex, for graciously letting me have the colors and mediums of their products to use for the paintings in this book. And I wish to thank all of the people whose portraits appear between these covers; I would have been hard-pressed to write this book without a cast of players.

ACRYLIC PORTRAIT PAINTING

Introduction

For twenty-five years I've been in partnership with oil colors; it's been a thrilling, at times frustrating, relationship. And after living and working with this medium for so long, I've been able to predict every move it makes. To say that oil colors and I are compatible is an understatement; this medium has been good to me in my struggle to put people's faces on canvas.

About seven years ago, I—along with many others—was introduced to a new medium: *acrylics*. It didn't spell the end to my relationship with oils; I merely made acrylics a new member of my little firm. This junior partner has now attained such stature that I wanted to write a book about it. This book will tell you what I know about acrylic, its characteristics, and how I use it.

However, this also happens to be a book about portraits. I felt, then, that I had to go into all the essentials of portrait painting that I first explored in oil colors. The basic principles of painting a plausible interpretation of any subject have never changed, no matter what medium is used. These principles certainly can't be denied; they're the same ones used by anyone who wants to record life on a flat surface.

And so, while the medium may be a new one, the trip it's making is centuries old.

Helen Van Wyk
Rockport, Massachusetts

Chapter 1

Acrylic Painting Materials

The study of creative art theories and aesthetic points of view can ignore materials —but a study of the painting craft *must* include them. This is why it's important to provide the painting student with a description of the characteristics, possibilities, and impossibilities of his painting medium.

This book is all about acrylics—the newest painting medium. You'll find that learning all about your materials will free you to concentrate on the art of painting: putting your materials to use with taste and judgment for the sake of a good picture.

This chapter will define acrylics for you; Chapter 3 will give you the opportunity to acquaint yourself with them through a series of exercises. You know, of course, that you can't learn to swim without getting wet; the same applies to painting with acrylics.

This book is not only about acrylic painting; it's about portrait painting, too. The sound painting principles that guide me when I paint from the model are the same principles that apply when my models are vases, flowers, or landscapes. The key to handling acrylics is the same as handling oils: adjust to its characteristics.

In this era of instant everythings, the student expects instant success with acrylics. But take it from someone who knows, there's *no* magic medium. Painting —in *any* medium—is hard work, but it's also the most enjoyable, satisfying hard work I know of.

ACRYLICS DEFINED

I've seen a few books on acrylic painting, and they've gone into detailed descriptions of the chemical composition of the paint and mediums. This, I feel, has helped compound rather than alleviate the confusion. What possible use is knowing the chemical formula for the binding vehicle? How can knowing the pigment content of these paints help you paint a better picture? The *only* valid information about pigments is which ones are *transparent, opaque, warm,* or *cool.* Neither should you worry about permanence, as so many do. This is in the manufacturers' domain; I trust them and so should you. Save your concern and anxiety for the painting process.

To begin with, let's clear the air about one of the fallacies regarding acrylics: *no special pigments are used!* They're the very same as those used in all other painting media.

To further clarify this, I'd like to describe briefly what artists' paints are: they're pigments held in *suspension* by liquid binding vehicles (as opposed to dyes, which *dissolve* in *their* vehicles). Linseed oil is the binder for oil paints; a gum solution for watercolors; milk emulsion for casein; and for pastel, an aqueous binder that evaporates to leave a dry stick of almost pure pigment. Acrylic paints are pigments mixed with a liquid plastic binder.

In order to describe the many characteristics of the acrylic medium, I'll have to refer constantly to oil colors, watercolors, casein, and tempera. As much as I'd like to just "talk" acrylics, it's easier to describe them by comparison to their predecessors. But don't think acrylics will make them obsolete; we're just lucky to have one more medium to pique our interest. Today, we have so much; the old masters had so little and did so much.

FLEXIBILITY

Acrylics are the *only* water based artists' colors and mediums that are *flexible*. The other aqueous media—casein, egg tempera, watercolors—have a tendency to chip and flake, especially when applied heavily. This is why many of the painters of old used wood as their rigid supports, so they could underpaint in aqueous media for subsequent glazes. When they *did* paint on stretched canvas, their applications of tempera were thin enough to reduce the possibility of cracking.

When casein had its recent renaissance, its manufacturers were careful to caution artists to use only rigid supports. Andrew Wyeth, today's ultimate egg tempera painter, works primarily on firm supports. Watercolorists wouldn't think of applying their color heavier than washes—they know that any build-up of pigment will surely chip right off the surface. This is what makes acrylics so different; they'll flex with the movement of the surface they're painted on, and can withstand expansion and contraction caused by changes in temperature. And the artist doesn't have to concern himself with the thickness of his application.

ADHESIVENESS

Another feature of acrylics is their tenacious *adhesiveness*, and this greatly benefits the painter. While the oil painter has to be careful about making one layer stick to another, there's no such problem with acrylics. They'll adhere to any non-oily surface, and, as a result, to themselves. This relieves any concern about applying one layer (of any type) over another, opening the door to a wide variety of applications and a world of different effects. With this in mind, we wonder why so many beginners are stymied—even frightened—by acrylic paints. This is enough to reassure any beginner.

INSOLUBILITY

Acrylic applications are *waterproof* when dry. How can this help you? Obviously, it permits immediate corrections without disturbing the paint underneath, without muddying color, without having color bleed through to the surface. In an acrylic watercolor technique, details, delineations, and dark patterns can be set down; when they're dry, color can be washed over them without any fear of shapes moving or colors running.

This feature of acrylics once helped a student of mine out of a tight spot. She wrote to me, not long ago, about a picture she was working on for an important show. As is often the case, she was called away by the telephone's ring. She returned to discover that her three-year-old had done a thorough job with a tube of cadmium red light all over her new—and hopefully prize-winning—picture. The painting was rushed into the bathroom and immersed in the tub. The still-wet cadmium red washed away, leaving her painting intact; none of the colors in it moved at all.

We don't expect *everyone's* paintings to be "worked over" by toddling, budding artists, but it's nice to know that fresh errors can be washed clean without furrowing your brow about destroying all the creative manipulations under them. Because of a thorough understanding of her materials, this student knew how to react to mistakes and accidents.

RAPID DRYING

This medium dries very *fast*.

It seems that students are just as concerned with how acrylics dry on their palettes as on their canvases. There's a logical solution to keeping acrylic paint wet on your palette, if you bear in mind that only *thin* applications of acrylic dry quickly, because it dries as a result of evaporation. As soon as the moisture has been lifted out of the paint that's exposed to the air, that paint dries. That's why acrylics stay moist longer on humid days than on dry ones. Thus, if a little amount is squeezed out, that little is exposed to the air and dries rapidly. The way to overcome this is to squeeze out a *generous* mound of paint onto your palette. Where the air touches this "puddle," a protective skin will form on the outside and the color under the skin will remain wet and workable for quite awhile. *Don't break this skin!* Dig your brush *under* it, and pull fresh, moist color out into your mixing area. The skin's not waste—it's protection. Remember, acrylic paint in any sort of depth will stay wet longer—on your palette and on your canvas.

Keeping your paints wet on the canvas can also be done with mediums and additives. I'll tell you how a bit later on, when I describe each medium for you.

Right now, though, I'd like to cite how I put acrylics' fast-drying nature to use. I love the beauty of transparent color, and I find the chance to paint and glaze, then paint and glaze again in rapid order to be intriguing and rewarding. I use acrylics now as an underpainting for themselves *and* for my oils. I hated the drying time needed for the indirect, underpainting and glazing approach to oil painting, and hardly ever used it until acrylics came to the rescue of what I consider the grand way to paint in oils. The fast-drying acrylic color makes it possible for me to prepare "polychrome"—or complementary—underpaintings, over which I can paint with oils the same day. Or I just begin directly in acrylics and *finish* up in oils, since beginning layers of oil can be very unhandy to work on because they're wet.

MEDIUMS AND ADDITIVES

We've just dealt with the distinct characteristics of acrylic paint. Now, let's discuss the mediums and additives that can be used with the colors to alter their consistency and character in order to create certain specific effects.

So that you'll fully understand these constantly confusing mediums, I'd like first to catalog them for you:

Gesso functions as a primer and ground.

Modeling paste is an additive that extends the amount of color it's mixed with.

Gloss medium imparts more gloss to your color as it's thinned.

Matte medium makes your color less glossy as it's thinned.

Gloss varnish is for a final gloss coat.

Matte varnish is for a final matte coat.

Gel makes opaque colors transparent and makes any application a glaze.

Retarder slows the drying rate of wet colors.

GESSO

This is a pigmented (titanium white) acrylic substance that's flexible, waterproof, and adhesive when dry. Gesso is primarily a material to be used as a painting ground; it's not a medium. In comparison with the classic gesso grounds—a blend of chalk and hide glue—this acrylic version is less absorbent. It can be applied and then sanded for smooth painting surfaces, or applied in various ways to obtain textures.

Acrylic gesso makes it safely possible to prepare inexpensive fabrics, raw canvas, and any non-oily, rigid support as a painting ground. Chapter 3 tells you the many ways to achieve unique textures with gesso.

MODELING PASTE This, too, isn't a medium but an additive. Modeling paste is a non-pigmented material that combines acrylic medium and marble dust. Added to color, the paste will enable you to paint more thickly. It actually extends, or bulks up color because you end up with as much color as the amount of modeling paste used. The color, however, will lose none of its intensity, unless there's an unusually large amount of modeling paste mixed into it.

When wet, modeling paste can be textured with implements; when dried, it can be overpainted, carved into, and sanded for extra effects.

Modeling paste will also retard the drying time of your application because you deal with a thicker amount of paint. As you become more familiar with it, you'll be able to determine how much to use to control drying.

Finally, most acrylic colors on the market have a tendency to level or flatten out. Modeling paste makes it possible for you to paint impasto passages like the peaks on a lemon meringue pie.

GLOSS MEDIUM This liquid medium is produced by some manufacturers as a combination medium and varnish in one bottle, and by others as a separate medium and separate varnish packaged in two somewhat different forms. Even though you may have bought the combined product, we'll discuss it first as a medium, then as a varnish.

Many painters I know prefer to use only water as their medium. I agree with them. But there are some who want a high gloss finish to their work. Then they'll mix gloss medium into all of their colors. They'll further add to the sheen by coating the dried painting with an application of either the medium-varnish made by some manufacturers or the varnish made by others.

Gloss medium can be used for glazing. It extends the color much like a painting medium in oils. But it won't make an opaque color transparent unless the color is thinned with a great deal of medium.

When you use this medium as a final varnish, be careful to dilute it with 50% water, otherwise a slightly milky film will remain. You'll be left with just that—a milky film on the dried painting.

MATTE MEDIUM Here, too, this liquid material is available as medium and varnish in two bottles and also in combination in a single bottle. Its characteristics are precisely the same as gloss medium; the finish, though, is entirely different. Mixing great amounts of matte medium into your colors will give you a surface that has the chalky look of casein or pastel. A great many painters want this effect.

Although acrylic paintings don't have to be protected with a coat of varnish, you'll find you can add to the matte look by brushing this varnish (also with 50% water) over your dried painting.

GEL When gel—which is pasty and transparent—is mixed into any color, even opaque ones or those with white added, it'll make them transparent and they'll stay just as thick. This is a good glazing medium that many painters prefer because its consistency is the same as that of the colors.

Gel reduces acrylic colors' strong covering power and gives you an opportunity to apply tender, subtle layers of color and value. It's the answer to the blending problem in acrylic painting; paint mixed with gel will fuse more easily for soft transitions. Applications of color mixed with lots of gel can mute any harshness of color. I use gel to tenderize my applications and modeling paste to strengthen them. I start my picture with color assisted with modeling paste, and use gel in my color applications in the development stages and at the end of the picture. Layer upon layer of color mixed with gel will give an opalescent and enamel-like look.

RETARDER This is exactly what the word implies. It not only keeps your paint from drying on the canvas but on the palette as well. I use a retarder in the final stages, where little areas of blending are needed. Using it in the beginning defeats the whole purpose and beauty of the fast-drying acrylic medium.

This takes care of our discussion of the nomenclature of acrylics. The next chapter will familiarize you with my palette of colors, my brushes, and my studio equipment. Then, Chapter 3 is all yours; it's your personal, practical introduction to acrylics through a series of projects for you to work on.

Little Joey *Acrylic on Masonite, 20″ x 24″.* This painting was made up of only four values that were suggested by the lighting: the tone of the Masonite; the general tone—lighter than the Masonite; the shadow pattern—darker than the Masonite; and the tone of the calligraphy—my darkest darks. After a sketch was made, I painted with white where the light struck the hair, face, shirt, and arms, letting the toned surface act as the shadow pattern. Acrylic's fast-drying property offers great opportunity to apply glazes (transparent applications of color over a dry area). By the time I had brushed white on the arms, the upper part of the figure was dry. I then started to glaze with acrylic colors, mixing matte medium into each one: the hair, including the shadow side (raw sienna); the face (mixture of yellow ochre and cadmium red light); the shirt (phthalocyanine blue). After these areas had dried, I carefully drybrushed pure white over the light pattern, feathering the tone toward the shadows. Again, after a short wait for this application to dry, I glazed the entire picture with the same colors I had used in my initial glaze. My darkest darks, which drew the picture to its conclusion, were touches of calligraphy that I felt were essential in order to retain the small boy quality.

Chapter 2 My Studio and Its Equipment

A studio's primary function is to offer the lighting conditions necessary to paint an illusion of three dimensions on a two dimensional surface. One constant source of light that doesn't change presents the condition and contrasts to get the feeling of solidity in your painting. This is such an important part of recording a human likeness; after all, we *all* have one thing in common—we have weight and we take up space.

Your studio doesn't have to be elaborate, just well organized and *ready at all times*. The excitement of the painting process may make you messy, but a well organized studio, always ready for work, can weather the confusion and any disorder that arises. Furthermore, having to set up the studio for each painting session may dampen your creative urge before you get the chance to start.

My studio has high, medium, and low windows on the north side of the house. I control my lighting effects on the model with shades on the window and by locating the model close to the window for sharp contrasts, far from the window for more subtle effects.

I line up my model stand and easel in a way that makes observation easy. The model usually sits at my eye level, but I have various sized stools to view my model from different vantage points.

At all times, a mirror stands imperiously behind me; its reverse image tells me the true story of my picture's development. Along with my ever-present mahlstick —to rest my hand, to guide my stroke, and to keep me from staining the tip of my nose with fresh paint—I have a reducing glass to check my proportions further, and an indigo glass to check my values.

I can set up a studio almost anywhere, but one studio prop that's very personal is my palette.

MY TRAVELING STUDIO

Traveling to your model's home or office provides you with a new catalog of ideas. A portrait painter friend of mine will *only* paint his models in their own environments, always trying to include a personal item into his composition.

My traveling studio is compact and quite complete. Except for my palette and canvas, all of my materials fit into my sketch-box easel, whose legs fold and lock into the 12" x 16" box. And traveling with acrylics is easy. Every household has tap water and coffee tins for containers. In some cases, I also bring along oil colors, turpentine, and medium, which also fit into the box.

The only problem about painting on location is the absence of a model stand. I overcome this by lowering the easel to permit me to sit at eye level with my model. This has its drawbacks, because not only is it uncomfortable, but it also makes it inconvenient for me to step away constantly to check my picture from a distance. I remedy this with Polaroid pictures as I paint to check on how my painting's progressing.

MY PALETTE

So many beginners think that the palette is just a place to squeeze out color in any old way. Actually, my pictures are painted on my palette as well as on the canvas. The palette serves as a proving ground where my tones and colors can meet before they shock each other on the canvas. For this reason, I insist on a toned palette—for how long does the canvas remain white? Students try to mix values on white paper palettes to relate to the values of their subjects and their paintings after all the white canvas has been covered. This presents a difficult strain on the eyes' attempt to compare and record the tones and values in the painting.

Since acrylics adhere permanently to wood—and to almost anything—I had to search for another material to use as a palette. I decided on a medium toned, warm gray Formica, which I had cut to the size and shape of the wooden palette I've used for oil colors for twenty years. After my painting sessions, I run hot water over it, which enables me to scrape the color off with a razor blade. A pane of glass (with a sheet of medium toned paper under it) can also serve well as a palette for acrylics, but I believe in *holding* my palette, which I can't do with glass. I want my colors close to me when I'm working from the model, but I often put my palette down when I work on backgrounds or when I'm just filling in areas.

There are so many little patches of different colors in the face; if they can't be readily mixed on a hand-held palette, I may become lax and say it doesn't matter. Sure, the palette becomes heavy; and yes, I *do* get a numb thumb. But it's a small price to pay for the ease of mixing the colors for the many nuances of the face.

MY CANVAS

Canvas serves as the support for my painting. The paint doesn't change the surface, but simply rests on it in layers. The texture of the canvas eases my paint applications; I paint on very rough or very smooth toothed canvas, or on primed Masonite. I choose the texture to suit the manner in which I want to interpret the model: a rougher tooth for a soft, smooth effect; a fine tooth for a rougher, paintier application. (This may seem like a contradiction, but this is just the way it works out: the rough surface softens the stroke, which stands up on a smooth surface.) I prefer the resilience of a stretched canvas; I also enjoy working on the smooth side of Masonite that's been coated with gesso for a semi-absorbent surface.

Often, students paint more freely on a used, repainted canvas, because they're less inhibited by the risk of failure. It becomes a "what-have-I-got-to-lose" attitude. I *always* have that attitude, even on a brand new white canvas.

MY BRUSHES

Types of brushes have a bearing on a painting's texture. The way I handle a brush can aid in suggesting form. Generally, these are the brushes I use for painting portraits:

White bristle flats (long bristles): for massing in large areas.
Red sable brights (shorter hair): #4 to #20 for painting shapes.
Red sable rounds: for calligraphy and for painting smaller areas.

I clean my brushes with liquid soap and warm water (I *never* rub them on a bar of soap), and swish them in a container of water to flush the paint out from between the hairs. All this, of course, follows rinsing them thoroughly during the painting session. I've heard that denatured alcohol will remove dried acrylic paints from brushes; I've never had to use any because I'd never permit these valuable tools to fall into that deplorable condition.

As long as your studio is well organized it doesn't have to be elaborate.

My model sits on a stand at my eye level and in line with my easel.

Three items that help me: a mirror to give me a fresh eye; a reducing glass to check my drawing; and an indigo glass to check my values.

These two vases contain all the kinds of brushes I use. The vase on the left holds my specialty brushes, my wash brushes, and an assortment of blenders, for example. The vase on the right contains my brushes for general painting—bristles and sables of all sizes. During a painting session, place used brushes in a tray of water, not in a jar.

Ralph Entwhistle *Oil on canvas, 18″ x 22″.* This portrait is in sharp contrast to the one of Little Joey. Even though the light is coming from the same side, there's a different attitude because it's more sharply striking from above. This is an oil painting, which may seem alien in a book about acrylics. But I included my portrait of Mr. Entwhistle for two reasons. The first one is technical; this painting points out that no matter what medium you choose to work with, the factor and problem of lighting are always there. The second reason is personal and a bit sentimental, for Ralph Entwhistle was the first teacher I had, many years ago, when I decided to embark on the glamorous career of portrait painting. I'm now not too sure how glamorous this business is; I do know, though, that it's exciting and challenging. I felt that the man who first launched it should be represented in my book.

Clarence Hall *Oil over acrylic on canvas, 24" x 30".* The portrait painter has a problem that other painters don't have: he has to make a good painting and·get a likeness as well, all on command. This is why my own studio, as pleasant as it is, can't possibly be the environment for all of my portraits. Working in his studio, with a limited number of props around, the portrait painter must be careful not to use the same prop—a chair, a vase, a distinctively decorated drape—over and over again. Many times it's not the fault of the painter, who may unthinkingly place his model in an atmosphere that other models had previously lived in. I painted Clarence Hall in the library of his Philadelphia law firm. I can honestly say that I'd never have included the books if Clarence had posed in my studio. So, as much as I love to paint in my studio, a change of scenery can often spark me with new ideas. Collection, Clarence Hall.

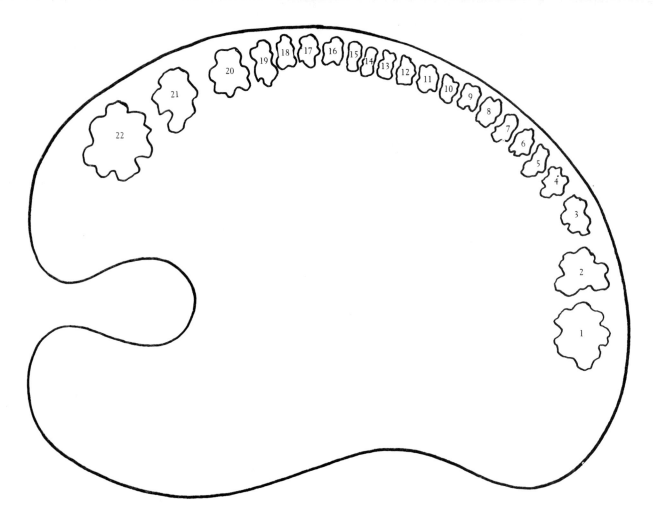

•1. Modeling paste
2. Titanium white

Light, bright, warm colors
3. Thalo yellow green
4. Cadmium yellow light
5. Cadmium yellow medium
6. Cadmium orange
7. Cadmium red light
8. Grumbacher red

Medium, bright, warm colors
9. Yellow ochre
10. Raw sienna
11. Red oxide

Dark, warm colors
12. Raw umber
13. Burnt umber
14. Burnt sienna
15. Mars violet

Cool colors
16. Thio violet
17. Thalo crimson
18. Thalo blue
19. Hooker's green
20. Thalo green
21. Mars black
22. Gel

This is a right-handed world, because only 10% of its population uses the other hand. This is my palette, a left-handed one. That's why you see white at the right and black at the left. If you're left-handed, this layout's just right; if you happen to be one of the majority, reverse the entire arrangement (black at the right and white at the left).

I like to hold my palette, because I want it in line with my canvas and model. I really paint my pictures on my palette, checking each value against each other before applying it to the canvas. In this cartoon by Herb Rogoff, the hand holding the palette looks kind of busy: it's gripping brushes, paint rag, and my mahlstick—which I cling to like Linus clings to his security blanket. Believe me, in actuality, my hand is that busy.

MY MEDIUMS   I use water to thin acrylic paints. I don't use the liquid mediums for general painting, but will use gloss medium to thin the paint when I want to lay in a wash or glaze a large area.

I add gel to my paint to make it transparent and glaze smaller areas, mostly in the development stages. For a more impasto type of application—to make the patterns of my brushstrokes show—I'll add modeling paste to my flesh mixture.

MY COLORS   The chart below will familiarize you with the characteristics of my colors. I've arranged them the way I do on my palette. Although there are sixteen listed, you'll note that they're actually *six* colors—yellow, orange, and red (the warm colors); violet, blue, and green (the cold colors). I've also catalogued each one's properties: *tone* (or value)—how light or dark it is; *intensity*—how bright or dull it is; *hue*—how the color deviates from its absolute place in the spectrum.

Tube Color	Hue	Intensity	Tone	Helpful Hints
Titanium white	None	None	Lightest light	In order to lighten colors and make them look illuminated, they need the addition of white. Not a color, only a lightening agent.
Cadmium yellow light	Spectrum yellow	Bright	Light	Somewhat cool; helpful in making warm greens when it's mixed with gray.
Cadmium yellow medium	Yellow orange	Bright	Light	Needed to make bright yellowish colors. Warmer than cadmium yellow light.
Cadmium orange	Orange	Bright	Light	The hottest color, because its hue deviation can't possibly be cool. Orange gets either more red or more yellow.
Cadmium red light	Red orange	Bright	Light	I can't seem to mix any flesh color without it.
Grumbacher red	Spectrum red	Bright	Light	It's so primary that it can be the core of bright warm color (cadmium yellow light is the other half); great with green to make gray.

This next group of warm colors are less intense, darker versions of yellow, orange, and red:

Tube Color	Hue	Intensity	Tone	Helpful Hints
Yellow ochre	Yellow	Medium	Medium	As indispensable as cadmium red light.
Raw sienna	Yellow orange	Medium	Medium	Very handy, but can be done without.
Red oxide	Red	Medium	Medium	As important as a bright red; like Venetian red or light red in oils.

A color loses its intensity as it drifts away from its tonal place in the spectrum. Thus, these next colors are very low in intensity, as well as being dark:

Tube Color	Hue	Intensity	Tone	Helpful Hints
Raw umber	Yellow	Dull	Dark	Shouldn't be confused with a dark tone and then used for a shadow; looks like mud if it isn't used only as dark yellow.
Burnt umber	Yellow orange	Dull	Dark	Good color to add to a flesh mixture when the intensity has to be reduced slightly.
Burnt sienna	Orange	Semi-dull	Kind of dark	A color found in nature, but can't be mixed; very transparent.
Mars violet	Red	Dull	Semi-dark	Can be done without; I seem to need it in my intermixes for background areas.

Now for the cool side of my palette. You'll notice that most of these colors are dark, yet intense. The cool colors of the spectrum are dark ones, so they're most intense when dark. These colors tend to get less vibrant as they get lighter. They can be lightened with additions of white; lighter, less intense versions can be obtained by mixing the cool colors with gray.

Tube Color	Hue	Intensity	Tone	Helpful Hints
Thalo crimson	Red-violet	Intense	Semi-dark	I wish this color could be darker in value; it's no substitute for alizarin crimson.
Thio violet	Blue-violet	Intense	Dark	Loses its intensity easily when mixed with white; beautiful when mixed into darker flesh to impart that diffused, shadowy look.
Phthalocyanine (Thalo) blue	Blue-violet	Intense	Dark	As necessary as red because it's primary. I like this color; it's the darkest and most brilliant of the blues. Lighter and less intense variations can always be mixed.
Phthalocyanine (Thalo) green	Blue-green	Intense	Dark	No combination of yellow and blue can make this beautiful, intense green.
Mars black	None	None	Darkest dark	Use with degrees of white to make tones of gray. Add a warm color for warm gray, a cool color for cool gray. In oils, I use ivory black because it's the most transparent of the blacks.

My palette of colors, organized in this fashion, will help you to dip into the ones that answer, or come close to answering these questions, which you should learn to ask yourself:

What color do I see? One of the six spectrum colors.

What tone is it? Either light or dark. This is a relative quality.

What intensity is this toned color? The color is bright or dull.

What hue is the color? The red, for example, is more violet or more orange.

Let's take an example. The flesh color is where the light strikes, so you must use white. The flesh color looks bright red—add cadmium red light to the white. That mixture looks too red—add yellow; but since the yellow of the skin looks duller than cadmium yellow, add yellow ochre instead. Then try the mixture out, and adjust its hue—more red or more yellow. It it looks duller, add a duller yellow, orange, or red. If you see a color that you describe as a gray-blue, mix gray and add blue.

Understand what you actually see. Your observations of this colorful world must be reduced to paint that can be one of the six colors of the spectrum, further identified by its hue, tone, and intensity. Your paint has these properties, as the chart of my palette shows. Paint doesn't have the properties of hair, flesh, or clothing. Black hair isn't black paint, flesh isn't flesh paint, blue eyes aren't blue paint, nor brown eyes brown paint. The colors on your palette give you a chance to present an *illusion* of light's affect on these objects.

Finally, here's a generalization of what flesh color is: any warm color into white. We see flesh color only where the light strikes the face. Shadow flesh is any warm color into gray or darker, duller, warm colors; or it's a flesh mixture with less white and then toned down with a complementary color—violet, blue, or green.

Color from the tube painted on canvas.

Color from the tube painted on watercolor paper.

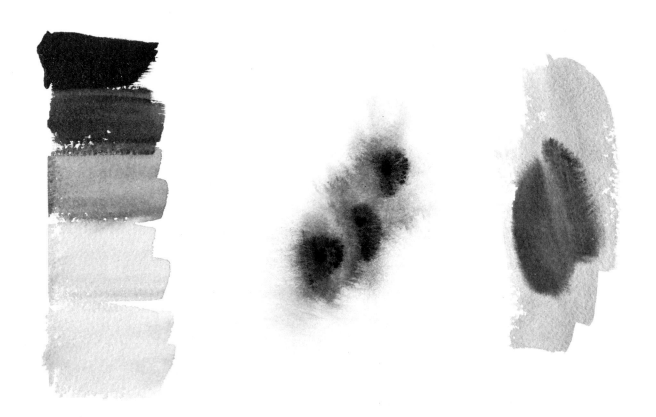

(Left) Color made progressively lighter in value by the use of more water. (Center) Painting color onto wet paper. (Right) Painting color onto wet color.

Chapter 3

Exploring the Characteristics of Acrylics

Now that you've learned about acrylic paints—as well as their mediums—it's time to put them to use. Rather than paint complete compositions or even definite objects at this point, you may find that you can familiarize yourself more quickly by running them through a series of exercises. In this way, when you decide that you're finally ready to plunge in, your entire procedure will be fortified by the knowledge that came from this preliminary experience with the materials. (Don't discard any of the samples produced by your excercises; you'll be needing them.)

The bulk of this book contains demonstrations in which I'll illustrate various techniques. These will further solidify your understanding of acrylics.

PROJECT 1:
USING WATER
AS A MEDIUM

Acrylic paints have appealed to so many people in so short a time because they're water soluble. In so many homes where only small corners of rooms can be devoted to painting—and where normal living goes on all around the easel—turpentine, oils, varnishes, and their myriad odors have sent non-painting members of the household scurrying for sweeter smelling locales. Odorless acrylic paints need only water and water based acrylic mediums, all equally odorless. And they clean up with just plain water before they dry.

Squeeze some paint out of the tube onto a pane of glass or onto a paper palette. With a large bristle brush, paint an area of color on canvas and on a piece of paper to get the feel of the color's covering ability. You'll also get the feel of the water as it dilutes the paint. Then, try the same thing with flat and round (pointed) red sables. Although this exercise may seem very basic, it's important; it's advantageous for you to get the feel of water as the medium, since you'll be using it at least 75% of the time. You'll also discover that acrylics don't dry as rapidly as they're said to. Experiment with varying degrees of water to establish for yourself the relative drying periods for each.

Rinse your brushes thoroughly in clean water. Slosh them vigorously and you'll be surprised at how easily the color comes out of them.

PROJECT 2:
ACRYLIC AS
WATERCOLOR

Water added to the paints disperses the pigment particles. This is how thin washes of color are created. The following short exercises will introduce you to acrylic used as a watercolor.

Flat washes: Dip a brush loaded with water into your color and mix a wash. Then, paint it in a thin, flat application onto your paper. Repeat, but this time use more water. Do this again and again, each time with more water. Place each wash next to the previous one, creating a strip of color that gets progressively lighter. This will demonstrate how far you can dilute acrylic color with water. Try different colors—cadmiums, earths, blues, etc.; they all react in their own way to the water. (Hold the strips aside; you'll be using them for another exercise.)

Wet-in-wet: While it's true that acrylics dry faster than most painting media (at least those you've had experience with), you should find out about drying time for yourself rather than paying attention to statements you've heard and read without testing. You must realize, of course, that because acrylics dry by evaporation, the painter in Arizona will have problems that I, living on the ocean in Rockport, Massachusetts, won't have. In succeeding chapters, I'll discuss ways to live with this. Right now, though, you can learn for yourself how acrylics may be kept wet for use in watercolor painting.

Moisten a section of your paper with a wet sponge or brush. Paint some color into this wet area and see how it seems to spread and "bloom." Try less moisture; try more moisture. Check the drying periods for each as you work. You'll discover that acrylics don't have the tendency to dry "under your brush," as you've no doubt been hearing for so long. With this in mind, try painting wet color into wet color and study the effects you can achieve.

Wiping out color: When I decided to try my hand at watercolor painting some years ago, I went to my friend Arthur Barbour, an American Watercolor Society member, for some pointers. As a confirmed oil painter, the first thing I asked about was the white paint. "White paint!" he said, "You've got a whole *sheet* of it."

The watercolor purist wants the white of his paper to show through and function as the white paint he won't use. This is why wiping, scraping, blotting, and squeegeeing color away are all so vital to him. It's as easy to do with acrylics as with traditional watercolors.

Paint a wash of color and, while it's wet, wipe out portions with a rag or a dampened sponge; blotting paper will lift color, too. These materials will create soft effects. For a sharper, more precise pattern, use a square of cardboard and squeegee out the color, much as wipers do on an auto windshield. You can also use an old plastic credit card, a device that Edgar Whitney loves and recommends.

With acrylic, there's a way of correcting mistakes that's impossible to do with watercolors. Paint over the dried wrong color with a wide brush charged with titanium white. Stroke the area gently, but make sure that the white completely covers the error. After the white has dried, you can paint over it with the correct color, as if you're working on fresh paper, without any fear of disturbing the new, white, waterproof surface.

Graded washes and soft edges: Many painters employ flat color areas in their "hard edge" paintings. But we're concerned with injecting *dimension* into our pictures. This is done with hard *and* soft edges, achieved by blending or grading colors.

You'll find that you can make gradations of color more easily if you first dampen your paper. This will keep the color wet longer, giving you a better chance, and more time, to grade a wash successfully.

Paint a swatch of color with a large, round, soft hair brush (red sable or the less expensive oxhair). Rinse your brush thoroughly and then shake out the excess water. Starting at the extreme left of the swatch, run your brush over the lower third of it in a continuous motion to the right (if you're left handed, reverse the direction of your stroke).

Try it again, but this time make your brush even drier by wiping some of the water from it.

All these watercolor exercises will show you how easily acrylic colors are diluted with water, and will demonstrate the clean, transparent washes you can get with them.

Using a blotter to pick up color while the paint is still wet.

Another way is to squeegee it with a firm card.

Painting titanium white over your mistakes will provide a new surface on which to work.

Acrylics with a great amount of water will give you the same washes you can get with traditional watercolors.

To test waterproofness, color was applied on top of dried color and then, after the entire area had dried, it was scrubbed with water.

Color applied from tube (left) compared to color mixed with modeling paste (right).

PROJECT 3:
TESTING
WATERPROOFNESS

The previous exercises illustrated how you can "move" acrylic paints while they're wet. Another great advantage (mentioned often, but worth stressing) is how waterproof these paints are. This characteristic is by far the most important one because it can solve so many painting problems for you, and will also permit you to do things you couldn't do with oil colors—or with watercolors. (Succeeding chapters will show you how you can apply this feature to painting a portrait.)

Paint a square of color just as it comes out of the tube and put the square aside to dry; allow about fifteen minutes. While it's drying, go back to the strip of flat washes you prepared before for Project 2. Make sure that the strip is completely dry, then scrub a wet brush over the washes. The stronger tints (or washes) should remain waterproof, while the weaker ones should wash off. This destruction of the thinner washes is due to the dilution or extension of the binding vehicle to a point where its waterproof quality is all but destroyed. You may overcome this by adding matte medium (see Project 7) to the lighter washes. However, it's a good test to determine how far you can dilute your color with water and still retain waterproofness.

Now, take the square of color you've painted for Project 3 (which should be dry) and scrub over it with a bristle brush (made to take this abuse). Try nylon and oxhair brushes, even a wet sponge. If the color has been allowed to dry thoroughly, none of it will be affected by the water or by the vigorous scrubbing.

Lay another wash of a different color over these swatches; see how independent layers of color, one on top of the other, won't disturb one another and give a luminous effect. This is putting acrylic's waterproof qualities to good use.

PROJECT 4:
USING
MODELING
PASTE

Now that you've handled acrylics pure and in washes, it's time that you dealt with this versatile paint in terms of impasto painting—thick layers of color.

Oil painting has always attracted painters and collectors alike because of its "meaty" quality, especially where painted thickly. But oil paint—despite all the people who paint in this manner—was never meant to be applied in thick layers. Furthermore, this centuries-old painting medium has more rules and regulations tied to it than a girls' boarding school: art students are constantly being warned about starting with "lean" paint and finishing with "fat"; they're told never to paint fast drying colors over those that dry more slowly; and so on. The consequences of breaking these "rules" are cracks, peeling, etc., that students—and even more experienced painters—blame on the paint rather than on their method of applying it.

These problems don't exist when you paint with acrylics. As I mentioned earlier, you don't have to worry about the sequence of application.

The paints themselves can be built to *some* degree of impasto. But it's their nature to "level out" and not remain in the thick state in which they come from the tube. Some colors won't build up as thickly as others; these are the thinner, lighter, transparent colors, such as the phthalocyanines. Although chromium oxide green—an extremely heavy, opaque color—will retain its texture, the "peaks" will round off, giving it an artificial appearance, unlike oil paint.

Modeling paste (also called extender) is the key to impasto painting with acrylics. The following exercises will remove the confusion surrounding the use of this vital paste additive. They'll also guide your use of it in a painting and should, therefore, eliminate the wholesale abuse of this material.

First squeeze out a generous amount of cadmium yellow light and paint it in an impasto technique, letting your brushstrokes fall where they may.

Next, mix equal parts of modeling paste and cadmium yellow with a palette knife. Paint this new mixture alongside the yellow swatch without the modeling

A small amount of color mixed into a larger amount of modeling paste.

Gel painted over dried color with a firm bristle brush can give you interesting brushstroke effects.

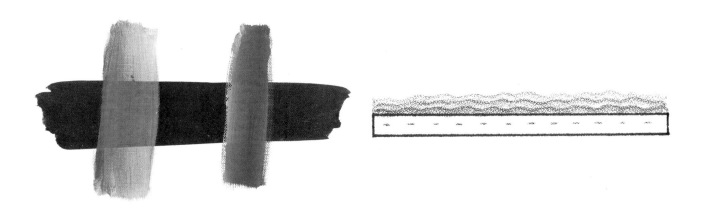

On the left, opaque color mixed with gel was painted over another color to show how gel makes colors transparent; right, opaque color without gel covers the ground color.

This diagram of a side view of a canvas illustrates how modeling paste should be applied in thin layers to obtain maximum effect.

paste. You'll notice that the modeling paste hasn't affected the color; it's merely given you twice as much paint as you originally had. You'll also notice that the impasto is sharper and more evident.

Larger quantities of modeling paste will lighten your color. Experiment with various amounts to determine just how much you can use without losing intensity. Mix a small amount of cadmium yellow into a sizable batch of paste. Compare it with the previous mixture.

The fact that modeling paste enables you to build up your paint to various thicknesses doesn't mean that you can run wild with it. Tube color in admixture with the paste—or the paste alone—has to be built up gradually, in ⅛″ layers, allowing each layer to dry before subsequent ones are added. This is strongly recommended; otherwise the paste under the surface will remain soft and pulpy for a very long period.

With a palette knife, apply the paste in a layer approximately ⅛″ thick; check the drying time. When that's dried, add another layer of the same thickness and again check the drying time. Build it up gradually in ⅛″ layers to a thick application. Alongside, spread one heavy application. Compare its drying time with the patch that was built up gradually with thin layers.

PROJECT 5:
TRANSPARENT
PAINTING
WITH GEL

The word *glaze* has, perhaps, confused more students than any other term in painting. Simply stated, a glaze is a thin, transparent application of one color over another. The glazing color, though, has to be absolutely transparent and this is where gel enters the picture (if you'll forgive the pun).

Many of our colors, in any medium, are transparent by nature: burnt sienna, the Hansas, the phthalocyanines, to name a few. Mars black, chromium oxide green, and the cadmiums are some of the opaque colors on our palette. Also, any color with white added to it will become opaque. Gel makes them transparent.

Paint a wide stripe of cadmium red light and put it aside to dry. Mix equal parts of gel and chromium oxide green. Don't be frightened by the milky color; this is gel's nature while wet, but it dries entirely colorless. Across the now-dry red stripe, paint the mixture of chromium oxide green and gel. You'll see the red show through the green.

Use the chromium oxide green without the gel and paint over another section of the red stripe, which will be *covered* by the normally opaque green. Now you see how gel can make an opaque color (like chromium oxide green) transparent.

Sometimes I prefer gel to the fluid mediums for glazing because its consistency is more closely related to that of the colors.

Another characteristic of gel is its ability to "set up" and form an impasto, like modeling paste. The difference, though, is that gel can be painted over a patch of dried color rather than mixed into it, because gel's transparent. Paint a square of color and set it aside to dry. Paint over it with clear gel, varying your strokes in interesting patterns. Use a firm bristle brush to get better brushstroke effects.

PROJECT 6:
GLOSS MEDIUM
AND VARNISH

As I pointed out earlier, some manufacturers combine the functions of medium and varnish (gloss or matte) in one product, while others market the medium and varnish separately. The exercises in this project are valid with either.

Without adding any water, mix some gloss medium into your color and paint a square. When it dries, the normally semi-matte (non-glossy) acrylic paint will now take on a distinct sheen. Because of the reflective quality of the gloss, colors will tend to seem brighter. Compare this swatch with the ones you painted earlier with water and with color alone.

Great amounts of gloss medium will serve you well as a glaze. Mix some into a color and paint over another dried tone. Compare its flow properties with gel, which you used for the same purpose. As you become more conversant with these materials, you'll be able to determine when to use one or the other for glazes.

Now, try gloss medium as a varnish—or try gloss varnish. Over one half of the swatch in which no medium was used, paint the gloss medium or varnish. Keep in mind what I told you earlier about diluting the varnish with equal amounts of water to prevent a milky film. As a medium, though, you may use it full strength in mixtures with paint.

PROJECT 7:
MATTE MEDIUM
AND VARNISH
By now, you've experienced the versatility of acrylics as far as textures, tints, and glazes go. There are also a wide variety of different surface finishes you can get with them . . .

> Color from the tube: semi-matte (non-glossy)
> Addition of water: matte
> Addition of gel: gloss
> Addition of gloss medium: high gloss

Matte medium mixed with the paints will impart a non-glossy surface, much like casein. This medium completes the catalog of surfaces available to you. Getting to know the characteristics of each medium will make your decision about which one to use less confusing.

Paint a square of color from the tube. Next to it, add a square (the same size) of color mixed with water. In the third square, paint color mixed with gel. Alongside that one, paint a square of color with an equal part of gloss medium. And finally, paint a square of color with matte medium. Mark each one appropriately and save these surface tests for future reference.

A glaze, which I discussed earlier, has long been thought of as glossy because, perhaps, of its popular association with ceramics. A glaze can also be matte (non-glossy)—ask any casein painter.

Matte glazes are applied the same as glossy ones. The prime requirement for both is a completely dry underpainting.

Over a swatch of dried color, glaze another color mixed with matte medium. Allow the coat to dry and glaze a third color mixed with matte medium over it. Select colors at your own discretion.

What if you want a surface that's not as "slick" as the one you get with gloss medium and yet not as "flat" as that with matte medium? In that case, mix the two mediums into your color for a semi-matte finish that has more life than the color used alone.

Matte medium can be further used as a final varnish—and there's also matte varnish. Here, too, it's recommended that the medium be cut with water when used as a varnish—to eliminate the milky film that may result.

PROJECT 8:
GESSO FOR
CUSTOM MADE
TEXTURES
I've already introduced you to acrylic gesso. Now it's time for you to try it yourself.

Again, gesso isn't a painting medium; its value is as a ground for your colors. It may be used as it comes from the container or tinted with any color you choose.

First, you can coat an unprimed (or raw) piece of canvas or Masonite with acrylic gesso to create a suitable surface on which to work. (A short napped roller will give you a smooth surface; a long napped one will give you a rougher texture.) There's definite economy here since unprimed canvas and raw Masonite are considerably less expensive than the primed canvases and ready-made panels

On the left, color from the tube; on the right, color mixed with gloss medium.

Acrylics offer a wide variety of surface finishes. From left to right: color from the tube; with water; with gel; with gloss medium; with matte medium.

sold in art supply stores. But more important, the use of gesso can open the way to a great number of interesting textures that are simply unavailable in manufactured painting surfaces. Try these.

(1) Brush or roll gesso onto a canvas board. Allow it to set for a short while and then run a comb down the length; it's important that the gesso isn't too wet, otherwise it won't hold the texture. Do the same with the comb across the width. You can use Masonite (untempered only), illustration board, wood, or any other rigid support as your painting surface.

(2) After applying a coat of gesso, lay a heavily textured piece of burlap over it. Gently press down to make sure that the gesso—drying, but not *dry*—has been impressed with the burlap texture; then carefully lift the cloth off.

(3) Cover your surface with gesso and then use a pointed instrument to draw your picture onto it. Here again, the gesso has to be permitted to set awhile—but not dry—to make sure that the image will be a definite one. Try a simple still life first. After the gesso has dried thoroughly, paint over it in washes of acrylic colors. You'll end up with a "thick" watercolor. Try this also with an addition of modeling paste.

(4) Experiment with other materials for texturing, such as sponges (natural and synthetic), mesh from old window screens, heavily textured cloths, and other items you may find around your home, studio, and workroom.

(5) Commercial illustrators, and some professional painters (especially those working in egg tempera techniques) prefer to use gesso in a very smooth manner. They sandpaper the gesso, apply another coat, let it dry, and sand it again until they end up with a glasslike surface. This permits them to work very tightly—to work with infinite detail. The illustrator can scrape away his mistakes and also achieve interesting effects by scratching into the gesso's scratchboard-like surface. Try this. You may enjoy using such a slick surface.

PROJECT 9:
FLEXIBILITY

Acrylic is the only aqueous medium that's flexible, and it may be safely painted on stretched canvas.

I hope you still have the tests from the previous exercises. Take those that are painted on paper and roll them up—loosely and then tightly. Do this with the modeling paste exercises, too. Generally, you'll find that acrylics are more flexible than other painting media. There are some brands of acrylic materials, however, that won't have the flexibility tolerance of others; you'll have to discover for yourself which ones are more flexible.

PROJECT 10:
BRUSH
TECHNIQUES

Now that you've become acquainted with the medium—acrylics—it's time to give some thought to the tools that transport the material from your palette to the canvas: brushes.

Despite the recent popular clamor for nylon brushes, *any* brush may be used for acrylic painting. As far as I'm concerned, the only advantage a nylon brush has over the others (those with natural hairs) is its easy maintenance; color *will* wash out more easily. But this should never be a factor in your choice of painting implements. I, personally, don't like nylons.

In the exercises you've already finished, you've used a variety of brushes; you've already experienced—I hope—the many things you can do with different types. We can consider the following exercises the specialty departments of the entire store of acrylic painting.

After the gesso had set (but not dried), the surface was textured by running a comb over it.

A coarse fabric, such as burlap, was pressed into drying gesso. When lifted off, the burlap's texture was in the gesso.

Scratching into the drying gesso with a sharp instrument will give you any number of interesting textures.

An old piece of mesh screen can be used to press onto the drying gesso for another intriguing texture.

A light opaque color was applied over a dried darker color to lighten the area. This is called a scumble.

Wet color was painted into wet color in a technique called *alla prima*—all at once.

Two ways to fuse colors. On the left, wet color was cross-hatched into another wet tone; on the right, fusing was accomplished by stippling color into color.

Using water to blend in an additional layer of color.

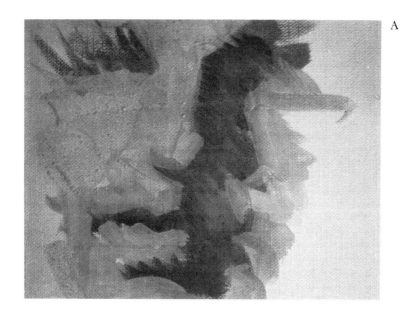

A

B

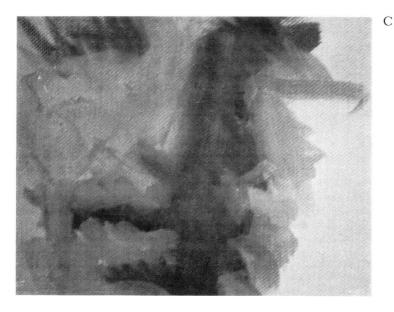

C

A demonstration of blending two tones: (A) the shape made, using two tones—light and dark; (B) breaking the shape with crosshatched strokes; (C) smoothing out the crosshatch with the brushstroke following the shape.

Scumbling: This, like glazing, has confused most beginning painters. Scumbling is the application of light and dark *semi-opaque* color over previously applied dried colors, using a bristle brush in a scrubbing motion. Scumbling usually is used to lighten and haze an area. (More on this in my demonstration chapters.)

Roughly paint a passage with chromium oxide green and wait for it to dry. With a firm bristle brush charged with cadmium red light (its complement), scrub thinly over the green. The cool undercoat should show through in spots, giving this passage a depth of richness difficult to achieve in direct painting. Try your own color combinations.

Alla prima or wet-into-wet: In Project 2 you painted with wet washes. Now, using color from the tube, paint undiluted color into wet color. You'll see for yourself the intriguing effects you get as colors mix spontaneously on your canvas.

Lay opaque tones next to each other and blend the edges together with a wet brush. (My alla prima demonstration number 9 shows its application to the portrait.)

Crosshatch and stipple: Although acrylic colors may be blended, some painters prefer to use them to simulate egg tempera. In this age-old medium, blending is all but impossible; tempera practitioners of yesterday and today have had to resort to crosshatching or stippling color into color to create an illusion of dimension.

Since a smooth surface works better, sand an application of gesso. Paint a rectangle with cadmium red light. Cover one half of it lengthwise with chromium oxide green. Then while the edge of the green is still wet, "feather" fine lines from it onto the red, using a small (#2 or #3) round red sable brush. Thin your color with water to improve its flow. Work your lines diagonally, first up and then down, to create tiny crosshatches.

On that same rectangle, still working with a wet edge of green (if it's dry, apply another coat) use the point of the brush to stipple fine green dots into the red. These dots should be more closely bunched at the juncture where the green meets the red and then should be more widely dispersed as they spread onto the red. The eyes of the viewer do the rest as he sees the edge turning to create dimension without blending.

I hope you've now had ample opportunity to work with the acrylic colors and their many mediums. Now, it's time for *me* to go to work and describe and demonstrate how all of these elements can be used to paint portraits.

Chapter 4

The Three Planning Components

As I mentioned earlier, this book is not only about acrylic painting—it's also about basic painting principles. You've already discovered how acrylics differ from other painting materials, but don't confuse a material's characteristics with the fundamentals of the painting process. Regardless of *what* material you choose for painting, or *what* subject matter you choose to paint, your picture will be made with the *same ingredients*.

SEVEN COMPONENTS OF PICTORIAL EXPRESSION
There are seven undeniable elements that I believe *all* pictures have, whether it's a portrait painted by Rembrandt, Picasso, or even a five-year-old child. I call these elements *The Seven Components of Pictorial Expression*. They're listed below in capsule form and I'll discuss each one in greater detail in this chapter and in Chapter 5.

1. *Motivation:* your inspiration.

2. *Composition:* the balance, unity, and variety of the space elements of your painting surface.

3. *Drawing:* a culmination of proportion, perspective, and anatomy.

4. *Rhythm of application:* application of a substance in some kind of thickness and manner.

5. *Tone:* the five tone values caused by one source of light.

6. *Found-and-lost line:* sharp or fuzzy peripheries that help to show projecting or receding planes.

7. *Color:* the factor in nature that can be used to dramatize and decorate the composition.

I've listed them separately to help you understand them more easily, but the seven components aren't separate—they're all interrelated. Naturally, from a technical standpoint, motivation, composition, and drawing have to be dealt with separately. I call these the planning components. It's only when you start to materialize with paint that you deal with the painting components.

When you begin to translate your ideas into paint, you do everything at once: you use a certain kind of rhythm of brushstroke, you get contrast with light and dark versions of color, you fuzz and sharpen edges for an appearance of dimension, and your applications vary in thicknesses. All this happens at the same time, per stroke. Of course, they're being piled atop your foundations of composition and drawing, and everything was put into action by your motivation, your spark of inspiration.

Stanley *Acrylic with modeling paste on canvas, 18″ x 24″.* A tall good-looking man, Stanley's even, strong features suggested a bold treatment of both lighting and brushstroke. Since his occupation was unimportant to his likeness, I painted only Stanley's head and shoulders. My motivation in this picture was obvious: my model was big and virile. I then had to use my materials to aid and abet what I wanted to get on canvas. I knew I would have to use broad, big brushes that would demand I observe the large masses so that I could set them down simply. Before I started to paint, I mixed matte medium into my modeling paste, and then added that mixture into all of the colors on my palette. This would assure me applications that were wet and juicy, enabling me to chop in bold patterns. The body tone was painted bigger than it is so I could cut the shadow into the wet flesh color. Of course, the shape of the shadow was carefully and accurately put in. The left periphery of the flesh area was cut in with the background, and then the flesh area was further developed with some simple statements of lighter tones of flesh. The lighting was strong, and from above, so all underplanes appeared very dark. Notice the darks caused on the lower portion of the eyebrows, the upper eyelids, the underplane of the nose, and the upper lip.

A tot with a crayon does this; obviously, he does it innocently. His scrawled product has a composition; it has a drawing, however incoherent it may be; it has a found-and-lost line as a result of his pressure on the crayon; and it has motivation—otherwise the child wouldn't have been inspired to make the mark in the first place.

Whether you're aware of it or not, you use these "building blocks" in every painting you do. Since they're the very nature of the painting process, why not study them and learn to realize how they can build a better picture for you? Every component can be put to better use if you know how potent each one is. *They transform an inspiration into actuality.*

Let's look at the planning components first: motivation, composition, and drawing.

MOTIVATION

Motivation has nothing to do with the actual painting process, but it's what puts the paint into action, the core of a picture's success. It's your attitude, your taste, your inspiration—a very personal reaction to things that then seek expression on the two dimensional surface.

Motivation is the spark that tempts you to make a paint translation. It provokes a concept that needs to find an identity. What you see is only a reference for this concept which has no form. This is the whole key, because there are no preconceived standards of what this concept should look like; it's what you want. When you begin to paint, the struggle between what you want and what you get begins. The wanting is the most important.

As a portrait painter, you have to paint what you want, not what you think someone else wants. So your model is only a point of reference for your original concept of him. This idea dictates the painting's style and will make the portrait more than a record of how the subject looks. It makes it a re-creation of the person in paint; it has the possibility of a good painting as well as a good likeness. Strive more for the former. After all, you're a painter first.

COMPOSITION

Just as motivation is the beginning of the concept, composition is the beginning of the *picture* of that concept. Composition—which I regard second in importance to motivation—is yet another of the seven components that make up the master plan, the construction of a painting. But none of these components can be isolated; each one is a vital link in the chain of good picture making.

The composition of a picture is its linear design; it's the placement of elements in a painting which form the very foundation over which the bricks and mortar of drawing, value, texture, and color will be built. This is the design of the subject on the canvas; it's an arrangement to pictorialize the subject, first in delineated design, then with form, contrast, and color.

ESTABLISH
THE COMPOSITION
FIRST

At this stage, a drawing of the head is still a premature involvement. Leave the drawing until later when you want to define the shapes you deal with. Composition merely indicates where the shapes are going to be. It charts the *direction* of the shapes, but does not delineate the actual shapes.

For example, if the body is facing left, just *indicate* this direction, without concerning yourself with the anatomy of the figure or with its clothing. All this can be attatched afterward by drawing over the already established design describing the body's placement on the canvas. You can't rush the painting process; first things must come first. Doing any intricate drawing at the compositional stage will only speed you away from this important element.

As an exercise, I ask my students to compose a still life that I set up in front

Paul Strisik *Acrylic on canvas, 20″ x 24″.* Paul Strisik's a very fine painter in Rockport, Massachusetts. In contrast to my portrait of Stanley, Paul's occupation was important enough to me to paint a portrait of him at work. Even though the features of his face are obscure, this is a good likeness of Paul. His personality impressed me to paint some areas in strong focus, and to cloud others in a mantle of mystery.

of them. After thirty seconds I say, "Stop," and they all groan. None was finished because each student had become involved with drawing, not with composition.

All you want now is simply the proportion of the head size. It's your first decision, so ask yourself: "What size should the head be?" Don't let this be an accident; establish the size of the head in relation to: (1) the size of the canvas; (2) how the model affects you; (3) your original concept.

HEAD IN RELATION TO SIZE OF CANVAS

If you're doing a portrait of a head and shoulders on a canvas large enough to hold life size (18″ x 22″ and over), here's an easy way to work within the framework of the canvas. Draw two diagonals on your canvas: from upper left to lower right; from upper right to lower left. They will cross at the exact center of the canvas. Keep the chin *above* the point where these lines cross; don't let it drop below the center. In this way, the head is in the upper half of the picture, and you can then make it life size, larger than life size, or smaller than life size. This system avoids your placing the head in the very center of the canvas where it'll look like a dartboard. Leaving more room at the bottom suggests a whole body under the head.

However, there's nothing wrong with centering the head on the horizontal part of the canvas, especially if it's full or almost full face. When painting a three-quarter view, a good general rule is to place the pit of the eye closest to you—the painter—in the middle of the horizontal axis of the canvas, again keeping in mind not to drop the chin lower than the exact middle of the canvas.

HEAD IN RELATION TO MODEL

Painting a likeness isn't merely re-creating the physical features of the model. I've seen portraits that were remarkable likenesses, but the subjects didn't look human. And so, when family members and friends of my model look at my rendition, I don't want them to say, "It *looks* like him." I want them to say, "It *is* him." Capturing the spirit of an individual requires more than facility with a brush; it involves serious study of that person, looking all the while for key points that will aid you in this dangerous caper you're trying to pull off.

I painted a doctor in Louisville, Kentucky, and had created a likeness in the initial stages of my composition. My model had a characteristic tilt to his head, which I captured before any features were set down; it was recognizable to all who knew him.

You have to relate to the model; that's the only reference you have. Too often, students just copy exactly what's before them without any thought of what they're doing, and they lose the personality of the person in the process. You wouldn't, for instance, paint a meek, mild person larger than life. You may even want to break a rule at this point and drop his chin *below* the center of the canvas, making his head smaller than life. This will intensify his meekness, obviously his most telling characteristic. On the other hand, a robust, athletic type of man, like John Wayne, calls for a painting *larger* than life.

Some years ago I did an interesting portrait of a woman who, every time she sat for me, stared at the ceiling instead of looking at me. As hard as I tried to direct her eyes off the ceiling, they'd look at me momentarily, and then go right back "upstairs." So I painted her looking at my ceiling. Some weeks after the portrait was delivered, I was at an exhibition and a woman approached and said, "Helen, that was a marvelous portrait of Mrs. Smith. She looks at my ceiling too."

As I did that portrait I could easily have ignored Mrs. Smith's ceiling inspections and I could have improvised the painting to have her looking at me. But observing her through the number of sittings told me that any attitude other than her upward gaze wouldn't have rung true.

This is the size of the head in relation to the canvas if you only want head and shoulders.

Size of entire composition in relation to the canvas if you include hands.

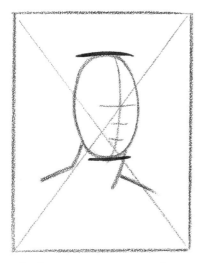

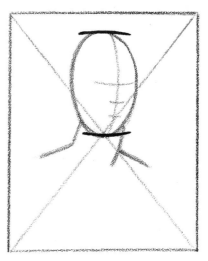

Two diagonals drawn on your canvas form an X at the exact center. When painting head and shoulders, the chin shouldn't dip below the X, as shown here.

The chin in this drawing is at the center line, making this a better composed picture.

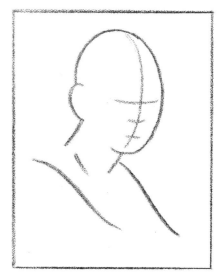

In a three-quarter view, placing the pit of the eye closest to you in the center from side to side (marked with an X), will give your picture more balance.

As you can see, this composition is wrong. Keep in mind that the difference between right and wrong is very subtle and requires close study.

Big Sam *Oil on canvas, 20″ x 24″.* Sam is my brother. He's six foot five and is tall even when he sits down. When he posed, he sat, folded his arms, and stared out at me. This was Sam; I painted him exactly that way. There's no ques-

tion that Sam's a big man. His head's smack in the center from side to side, the reason I chose this oil portrait for this book. What better way could I find to illustrate this important point of composition?

The Three Planning Components 49

Grandmother Packman *Acrylic on canvas, 10″ x 14″.* This marvelous woman was ninety-eight years old when I painted her. One might think that her portrait should have been more in keeping with her advanced age—a head smaller than life, for instance, to intensify her frailty. But I didn't see Grandmother that way, so I decided to paint her life size on a small canvas. This portrait is included in this section to show you how to compose a head on canvases smaller than 18″ x 22″. If you mentally draw an X through the center of the picture, you'll notice that Grandmother's chin dips well below it. If I had placed her chin in the center, the small head would have looked bizarre, and would have made Grandmother something she definitely isn't—meek and servile. Collection, Mr. & Mrs. Paul Iovan.

Perspective is vital to your composition and relates to the attitude of the model. Although you don't draw the perspective at this stage, you indicate it in your composition. How do you put this into play? A small child will look small if you look down on him; a proud person will look prouder if he looks down at you.

Where your picture hangs will also affect its perspective. Generally, you'll want to paint your portraits at eye level—that's the way most of them look when they hang on the wall. Knowing in advance where the portrait will hang in the home is a big help in composing it. Let's suppose it will hang on a staircase or high up on the wall. Then you'll want the model painted *above* your eye level.

So you see, composition sets the very pace of your picture. Get it wrong and you'll end up wasting valuable time piling the other components on top of it. Remember, your picture doesn't start with your very first brushstroke; it starts with a plan. The painting process only gives the plan substance.

HEAD IN RELATION TO YOUR CONCEPT

Composition can't stand alone—it must rely on other components. Motivation, as stated earlier, strongly influences your composition of the picture. This is your idea, your concept of how you want your model painted. The model's attitude has already dictated some of your procedure.

Now, armed with this ammunition, you must pose the model. Arrange him according to your taste, and once he's set and assures you that he feels comfortable and natural, don't let him deviate. He's modeling for you, and you've got to be dictatorial and cold-blooded about it. If he shifts position, get him back to the one you started with. You can't begin to improvise on your original design. If your portrait ends up looking awkward and unnatural, you can't say, "That's the way he sat." It should be your decision all the way. You can develop this cold-blooded attitude by practicing on still life, which will make you recognize how important it is to relate to the model as a point of reference rather than as a point of personality.

LIGHTING THE MODEL

After you've decided how you're going to delineate the pose and how much you're going to include, the second most important factor is the consideration of lighting. The painter doesn't paint the model, he simply records the lighting conditions on the model. He has to make his paint do what the light does. Make sure the lighting presents a good view of the model and a strong composition for your picture.

BALANCE, UNITY, VARIETY

Good composition is a combination of three factors: balance, unity, and variety. They're important in establishing a solid base for your picture.

Balance is a factor in nature and is the key to a natural composition. You can *look* at the distribution of your space elements to determine how they're balanced on the canvas. This, however, may be a bit difficult for the untrained eye. A better, more practical way to check balance is to *physically* balance the canvas in your hands. This sounds absurd, doesn't it? We all know that the elements on your canvas have no weight. But in a way they do. Hold the canvas flat and place the fingertips of one hand *under* where the head is on the canvas. This should be your focal point, and if balanced properly in the picture, the canvas should be able to rest rather flat or horizontally on your fingertips.

Let's suppose your hand is under the head which you had planned to be in the upper left of the painting. Your canvas will tip towards the right, which means that you should put something in that area to lift up the corner. The color, shape, or tone you intend to place in that corner are represented by the fingertips of your other hand. This balance that you're trying to achieve is actually what the

Portrait of Pearl *Acrylic on canvas, 30" x 40".* I started thinking about this painting ·the minute I received the commission. It was to be a large portrait of a woman engaged in a variety of social activities, and always on the move. This, plus her clothing and surroundings, was so much a part of Pearl's likeness. My main concern was how to treat the large areas of clothing and background; this is where my many years with still life were put to great use. The white mink coat suggested a feeling of light-toned atmosphere. The rough-toothed canvas I used "pulled" the paint off my brush, enabling me to drag it over the surface in order to impart this light look over-all. In any portrait, the percentage of face compared to clothing and background is small indeed, is the backdoor to portrait painting. Set up a still life with drapery as a background. Just as this is a painting of a woman, not of a mink coat, make sure that people see it as a still life with drapery, not the other way around. Collection, Mr. & Mrs. W. Feder.

eye of the viewer sees, and this is merely a device to use to double check what you've already composed. Obviously, you can't do this with a blank canvas to determine your composition; but you can do this after you've sketched in the major elements.

The second factor, *unity*, is the design of all the factors that relate to the person's countenance. If he's a very elegant individual, try to arrange everything in the composition—background, clothing, the pose—in relation to elegance. A casual person should get a casual pose and setting.

Injecting *variety* into your composition will prevent your picture from looking monotonous and tired. Place a dark-haired person against a light background; a light-haired person against a dark background. A brightly colored complexion can stand a bright background; but a sallow complexion will look even more sallow if placed in front of a bright background.

When painting folds in clothing don't make any two folds exactly the same; don't make two curls in the hair alike either. In other words, don't make any two areas of one thing exactly alike. There's a temptation to do this; you do one thing successfully and you want to repeat it. Make a new observation rather than repaint a past success.

A nice composition is a beautiful arrangement of balance, unity, and variety of all elements that you deal with. They're not single elements of hair, clothing, background, but an integration of elements to blend towards a better, more meaningful painting.

RULES IN COMPOSITION

Composition isn't a rigid component, certainly not as rigid as the laws of perspective which *demand* adherence. There's flexibility in composition. The rules, if I may call them that, can be broken but they should always be based on good judgment and good taste.

There are rules, however, that are absolutely inviolate. One of them is what I called "amputation." This means cutting a body off at the edge of the canvas at a point that's clumsy to the pose, the mood, and the general appearance of the model. When doing a portrait with a portion of the body in view, never cut the body, arms, or hands at intersections or joints. Don't cut at the elbow, wrist, or knuckles of fingers; don't cut at the middle of the breast line—male as well as female—or at the waist. Choose an area above or below these natural joints in order to avoid making your subject look like an amputee.

Another point to keep in mind is to avoid equadistances. Don't place the shoulders equadistant from the edges of the canvas; don't have the space element of the background the same on either side. If you're going to vignette the body, don't cut it off straight across; let some dramatic tones continue down into the haze at the bottom. And the top of the canvas to the head shouldn't be equadistant from the point of the body you're vignetting.

After years of painting professionally and years of teaching, I've arrived at the conclusion that students will tread where professionals dare not go. A good example in portraiture is the great number of meaningless, badly painted, ugly hands that show up in so many beginners' portraits. Why paint a hand, or hands, if they aren't necessary? Of course, if your sitter is a violinist, a pianist, or a surgeon—professions in which the hands of the subjects are part of their likenesses—you'll *want* to paint them. Anyone else, though, can be painted without hands. Don't paint what's unnecessary merely to embellish your picture. Nothing looks more ridiculous than a portrait with hands that don't know what to do, or don't know what they're doing there in the first place. If you must paint hands, make sure they're placed in a plausible position, not in a way that makes them look like clubs. Chances are if they look funny in the pose they'll look funny on canvas.

Composition, then, is more than merely linear design—it's the vital organs of the picture to make the picture breathe and live. I've set down many rules under composition, but please don't consider them absolute dogma. Just let them be a guide for you to aid you towards a more meaningful portrait.

DRAWING

Composition is the blueprint of your painting, drawing is the beginning of its physical construction—the 2″ x 4″ studs. The abstract element of composition needs the drawing to give it identity, to shape and define it; to make a particular person out of the compositional markings; to give that person a gender; and to give you a definite indication of what your over-all picture's going to be.

The painting process is difficult enough, so why make it *more* difficult by trying to *draw* with paint? You *draw a drawing and paint a painting.* When I say this to my students, I get looks of enlightenment. This is your first step to understanding the role drawing plays in painting. After all, you're working with thick stuff on your palette—globs of paint—that have to be transferred to canvas. You can't *draw* with paint, don't try; *paint* with it. The picture is made with paint; it's not a colored drawing. This is the key to recognizing that drawing in painting is a factor to utilize for the sake of the painting process.

As I said before, it's hard to separate the components in the painting process, but let's see what we gain by pulling drawing out of context. We need some guideposts to secure our paint. These linear indications must be set down to act as security measures for the paint application. But you really have to get the drawing as you paint, because a beautiful, accurate drawing, very carefully drafted, could inhibit the painting process. It becomes deliciously tempting to "color" this drawing rather than to paint a painting.

Accept your manner of drawing; it's personal, just like your handwriting. You can't write a word until you learn that word, so what is your "drawing writing" trying to say? It's trying to say three things: *proportion, perspective,* and *anatomy.* These can be learned, and once they become a point of knowledge, the hand performs better, because it knows what it's trying to do; it knows what "words" it's trying to say.

PROPORTION

Good drawing comes only from practice; it can't be taught, only criticized. A good drawing emerges from the act of drawing, because only then can it be criticized by someone else or by you. You have to develop a good eye to see what has gone wrong with your drawing, and above all you should look for proportion.

Proportion is so important that I really don't know how to stress it sufficiently, except that you just can't draw one area of your picture without comparing it to another in order to get it in the right size relationship.

Many people interested in painting portraits read books and lodge definite proportions in their heads. In most cases, these proportions are presented as formulas. The books tell you that the eyes are one-half the entire head from top to bottom; that you can divide the head in thirds: the hairline to eyebrows equals the eyebrows to the end of the nose which equals the end of the nose to the chin.

I don't believe in these formulas for proportions, because maybe you'll want to paint a person with his head down or up. All these proportions will then change, won't they? Or maybe the model has a very high hairdo—that changes the formula again. Maybe the model has a long nose and a short chin—that also changes the formula. You can't get the proportions of a person by stuffing him

To find the basic proportions, use a caliper to measure from the top of the head to the eyes in relation to the distance of the eyes from the chin. Measure the width of the head in relation to the height.

into a formula that was established to deal with all heads in general. You have to look at each one as an individual: that person's forehead in relation to *his* nose, *his* mouth, and *his* chin. As soon as you have a formula and you work according to *its* precepts, your picture's on its way to ruination because you're not aware of the model in front of you. And if you miss your proportions at this stage, you'll *never* get them right.

I feel that proportion is the most important factor in drawing. It defines the size relationship of one thing to another and also to itself. This means how tall it is in relation to how wide it is; or how large one area is in relation to another.

There are certain basic proportions of the face that are universal truths. Anyone can improve his drawing if he takes these things into consideration at all times: never do the forehead without mentally measuring its size in relation to the hair area; don't ever do the forehead without thinking of the size in relation to the eye area; don't put the nose in without thinking of how it's measuring up to the cheeks and the jaw.

Proportioning—or getting the proper proportion—is more a matter of being good at fractions than at being good at art. I hate to say that there's arithmetic in the art of painting, but this is fact. You mustn't worry about the mark your brush is making, but about what that mark indicates. It's mainly indicating size relationships of one object to another.

If you start with the nose, you can paint the whole picture and get it correct if everything else in the head is related to it. But if you think of the eyes and the mouth as independent elements, not related to the size of the nose, everything's bound to go wrong. In painting it's important to keep in mind that something *must* be put down, and then the creative venture stems from your relation to it.

Once you decide on the head size—a factor of composition not drawing— relate everything to that size. Then, line up your brush in midair along the line

Navajo Girl *Acrylic on canvas, 18" x 24".* You can aim your paint with great accuracy if you know where you're going. Before I begin to paint I measure all the elements of the head (shown in inset). Painting a portrait is like walking a mile; you must do it step-by-step.

that makes up the shape, such as the angle and line of the arm. Its angle, let's say, intersects the ear. Since the ear is in place, because you've already drawn it in, relate the line of the arm to it.

PERSPECTIVE This is the word that defines the linear way to record the illusion of dimension on a flat surface. Linear perspective describes how an object looks in relation to your eye and to the end of your sight. This is called the vanishing point.

Aerial perspective describes how tones and colors change in relation to their nearness or their distance. You hardly have to think about this in portraiture, except when painting backgrounds.

Perspective in portraiture means conveying the way in which the model looks from your vantage point, and how the shapes change accordingly. All the features of the face will be different as you look up at the model, look down at the model, or if you have him at your eye level. Many of these factors are parts of composition, such as making children look more like children if they're below your eye level. This is a good example of how interdependent all the components are.

I've found that the art of painting forces the painter to question himself constantly. The student picks up his brush and puts it to the canvas with only blind faith. It takes more than that. Even a carpenter hammering a nail questions himself: "What's the grain of the wood? Is the wood hard or soft? Is this the right type of nail for this job?" The painter must do this too. Ask questions of yourself; the answers are there merely for the asking: "What view am I seeing? Am I looking down on the face or am I looking up at it? Do I see it full face, or is it three-quarter?"

It's obvious that the subject sitting before you holds all the answers. A preconceived idea of an image ruins a true observation. You end up drawing what

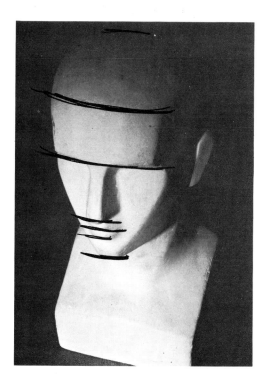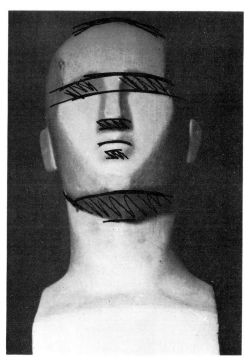

(Left) I've found that one of the ways to teach perspective is by stressing proportion. As you can see, a view of the head from a high vantage point changes all the basic proportions seen from a lower point. How, then, could there be a set formula for proportioning the head? A good drawing can only result from a keen observation of the subject. (Right) A view of the head from a low vantage point exposes all the underplanes. Again, proportions you may have used in another attitude are meaningless here.

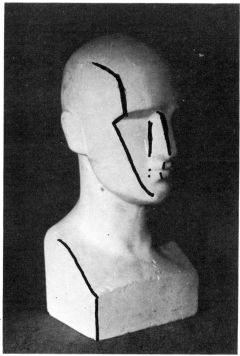

There are two types of perspective to help you to transform a flat surface into reality. *Linear perspective* alters the sizes and shapes of the planes of the face. All the planes that recede from the plane closest to your point of vision will reduce in size. All the side planes on the left are in line with your vision. On the right, the corner of the left side plane and front plane is in line with your vision.

Aerial perspective changes the colors and values of surfaces as they're viewed in space. It's easier to get a feeling of perspective by arranging your light for the shadow to fall on the receding plane, as in this portrait of Paul Iovan (12″ x 16″). In the sketch pictured below, the light was reversed—the shadow falling on the advancing plane—which makes it more difficult to create a dimensional effect. Collection, Mr. & Mrs. P. Iovan.

you *think* it is rather than what it *actually* is. You may have a vast storehouse of theoretical perspective, but you'll find that in portraiture it becomes a costly luxury, like owning a yacht in the State of Kansas.

I've always helped students more with perspective by stressing proportions rather than vanishing points. It seems more logical and, what's more, it gets results.

Here's a good general rule: think of objects closest to you being larger than those which are farther away. As a result, for example, the eye closer to you will be a longer shape laterally than the other eye.

Let's take another example: there's a painting of two men on a street. The man standing in the foreground is larger than the one in the background. So you say: "Look at that marvelous perspective." But it's not a matter of perspective that created this illusion, it's a matter of proportion. The man in the background —although the same size as the other one in reality—is smaller in the picture.

Perspective distorts the proportion of objects more than anything else does, evidence that proportion is the most important drawing elment. In pointing this out, I find that I succeed in helping the student understand perspective and its functions more easily—a very difficult concept to grasp.

Now, let's put perspective into use. After you get the over-all proportions of the head—how wide in relation to how high—make a line to indicate the dissection of the left or right side of the face. This line gives you the view you're looking at: full face, three-quarter, or profile. Put the line down strongly when you do the drawing; it's a construction line that eventually will be covered with paint, the line you'll relate to. The line establishes the symmetry of the face: how the jaw facing you looks in relation to the side farthest from you; how the cheekbones are; what happens to the anatomy of the mouth. In full face the mouth area is a round shape; in perspective—as it moves away from full face—it becomes an oval shape. The nostrils, eyes, everything that's round, is affected by the angle of the head.

Think of the head as an egg. If you look down at it, all the features are on a downstroke arc; they're straight if you look directly at them; and they're in an upswing arc if you look up at them. Indicating this will set the pace for the work to follow. With perspective you'll embellish what you initially established when you composed the head on canvas.

Perspective, then, is the linear implement that permits you to begin the illusion of three dimensions in the evolution of your portrait.

ANATOMY You're a walking anatomy book; all you have to do is feel your face. Knowing the names of the bones and muscles won't make you paint them any better, but feeling them will help you to recognize where they are and how they work.

I always felt that a person interested in painting portraits would be better off modeling a head in clay rather than pouring over a score of anatomy books. This would give him an appreciation and an awareness of solidity. Not only must the head you paint have a feeling of solidity, it must also have the feeling of the universal truth of all people—it must look human.

Let's suppose you're painting Mary Smith. Well, first off it must look like her—that's the job you set out to do. But Mary Smith's important as a human being; she belongs to the species, doesn't she? This means that people who don't know Mary Smith have to recognize her as a member of the human race, since her likeness alone means nothing at all to them. You can do this by paying close attention to Mary's anatomy, not just her surface likeness. I've seen portraits—and I'm sure you have, too—that look just like the people who sat for them. But they didn't look human. It was easy to deduce from looking at them

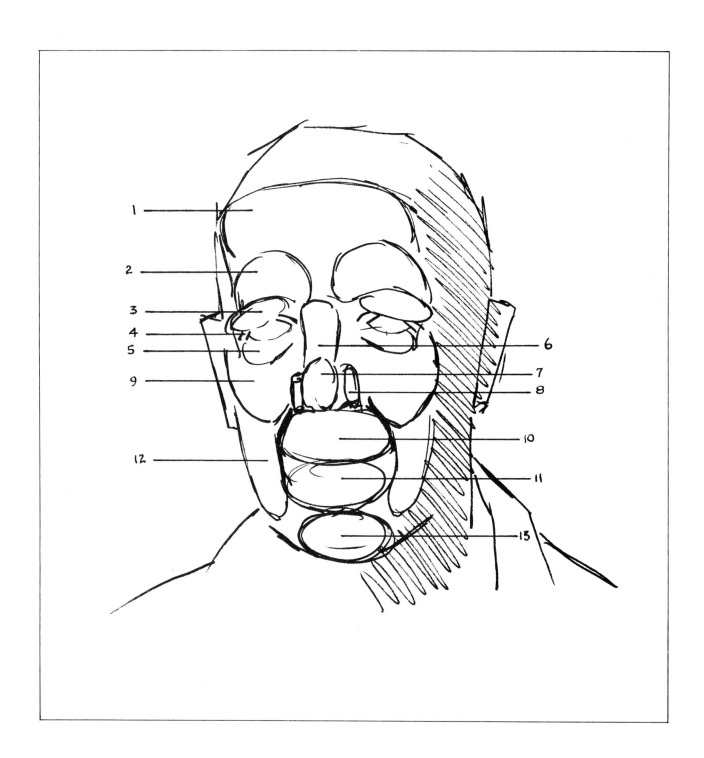

Anatomy, the third property in drawing, is the construction of the forms; a refinement, let's say, of the planes. I've divided the head into thirteen general areas: (1) upper part of the forehead; (2) lower part of the forehead, known as the brow; (3) fullness of the upper eye area; (4) upper eyelid; (5) eye itself and the lower lid; (6) upper nose area; (7) ball of the nose; (8) nostrils; (9) upper cheek area; (10) upper part of the mouth area; (11) lower part of the mouth area; (12) lower cheeks, between the cheekbones and jaw; (13) chin. You'll notice I haven't mentioned the eyebrows themselves. They form automatically because they're the shape between 2 and 3. Don't paint eyebrows as hair; paint them as a value.

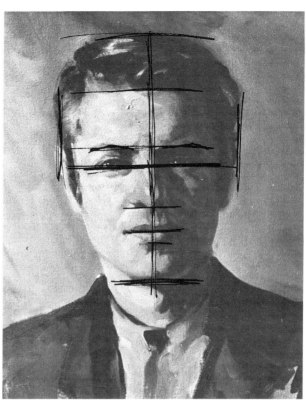

Here's how a knowledge of the three properties (proportion, perspective, and anatomy) can build a better drawing and result in a sounder painting. The finished picture.

With proportion superimposed.

With perspective superimposed.

With anatomy superimposed.

that the artist didn't bother to get beneath the surface likeness. Good drawing taxes your attitude toward anatomy—*any* anatomy.

When I studied with M. A. Rasko, my first lesson in anatomy was to paint an apple, one that was selected from a bowl of many. Rasko left the room and there I was stuck with a solitary apple when my real interest was in painting people. When he returned thirty minutes later, he didn't look at my easel but picked up the apple and threw it into the bowl with the rest. "Now I'll look at your picture," he said, "and from your picture I should be able to pick out the apple you painted." Of course, he didn't, because I didn't paint *that* apple, I painted a shallow observation of all "appledom." I relate this anecdote to illustrate the importance of being aware of anatomy at all times. When you draw it's not a mere outline; it's an indication of a construction. And construction is the anatomy.

You can best achieve solidity by respecting the planes of the face. In this case, think of the head as a box, and think of the over-all shape in terms of planes. You can find these planes with the palm of your hand. Place your palms against the sides of your head; these are the side planes. On them are placed the ears, the sides of the nose, and even the corners of the mouth which are actually on the side planes. Place your palm on the front of your face. This is the front plane, and on it are the forehead, where the eyebrows grow, the tip of the nose, the area under the nose, the front of the lips, and the chin. Then there's the top of the head, the only true top plane. But some eyebrows jut out and become top planes, and so do noses that tilt up. The top of the cheekbones are top planes, and also the upper ridge of the mouth.

Then the underplanes, so marvelous because light usually comes from above, throwing them into deep shadow. In the underplanes are the underparts of the eyebrows, the nose, the upper lip, and the chin.

So think of planes instead of thinking of the person. This is part of the anatomy, just as the five basic shapes the Chinese figured out long ago. The whole world, they said, was constructed of a ball, a cube, a cylinder, a cone, and a pyramid. Thinking of people in this way, and relegating them to these shapes, will make it easier for you to draw them.

Chapter 5

The Four Painting Components

You now know that composition plans the picture, and drawing further defines the composition. Now it's time to translate the subject into paint, and it's at this point that the fun and agony of painting truly begins. Now that the picture has been planned, it's time to paint.

RHYTHM
OF
APPLICATION

You no longer must think in terms of what your subject actually is, but how it will look in the very substance you work with. This is the hardest thing for beginners to do, because they think in terms of reality; they think in terms of skin, of hair, of fabric instead of thinking how to make skin, hair, and fabric out of paint.

Your rhythm of application is the very process by which the paint gets onto the canvas; it's the look of the paint as it's affected by its application with brush, painting knife, or whatever other implement you may want to use.

Rhythm of application isn't only the thickness or thinness of your paint, it's also the direction in which it goes. Without an intelligent type of application, one that holds together, the painting can be ruined. You can have a sound composition and a good drawing, but the painting will be unsuccessful if the paint is applied without any thought of its direction and function.

In order to understand what rhythm of application is, and the role it plays in your painting, dissolve all color and value out of the paint on your palette. This can be done by putting out a generous amount of modeling paste on your palette, and painting with this colorless substance. You'll be painting without the aid of color and value, an exercise that forces you to rely on the only component available—your rhythm of application. Whereas color and value can create the illusion of three dimensions in themselves, here you must create this illusion using *only* colorless "stuff" in a sculptural, textural way. This isn't done merely by applying thick or thin quantities, but also by the way you *direct* your brush-strokes.

If you think of the subject matter in terms of paint, you'll no longer just try to *turn* your canvas into a picture; you'll be using your canvas as a *support* for your picture. This is the true function of your painting surface.

Students grow timid when they begin applying their paint. Generally, they're reluctant to destroy what they've already established—composition and drawing—especially if these have been done well. Although you may become inhibited by the thought of covering your drawing with paint, it *has* to be covered, because —as I said earlier—the drawing only serves as the scaffolding for the painting.

In every art class I've taught, students stand—or sit—close to their easels, concentrating diligently on their drawings. They attempt to record their subject in perfect detail, line for line. Then, ironically, after they've completed their detailed

The impasto underpainting for the portrait of Vic (see color plate in Demonstration 5) shows the textural effect caused by the rhythm of application.

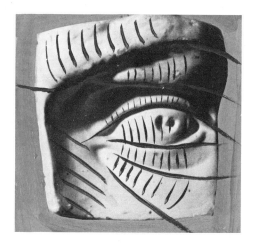 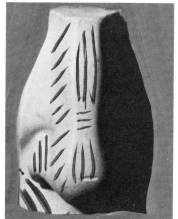 

The many little lines on the planes of the features show how the direction of brush-strokes can describe the direction of the planes.

drawing, they pick up their brushes and stroke paint on in an attitude of carelessness. They'll stroke from top to bottom, up and down, down and up, many times with strokes as long as six inches. I tell them that no stroke should be longer than 1½″; and every stroke should say something.

RHYTHM
OF APPLICATION
AND
PLANES

In portraiture, the planes of the face are painted with a rhythm of application that will give your portrait solidity and dimension. Stroke your paint on in the same direction as the plane. For instance, if you want the lower lip to protrude, pull your stroke *out*; if you want to make the front plane of the cheek come forward and the side plane of the cheek go down, actually apply the paint in this fashion.

There are shapes that follow the vertical planes and those that follow the horizontal. These two planes are obvious. The planes from front to back, however, are the ones giving the effect of three dimensions. These planes come toward you or go away from you. Your rhythm of application should pay more respect to them, to how you want these forms to project and recede.

Suppose you had to apply paint on a sculptured head. You'd follow each plane quite easily because you'd be working upon a solid, three dimensional object. Automatically, when painting the nose, let's say, you'd pull your stroke out, following the projection of that feature. Now translate this to the canvas in front of you; make your stroke in midair according to what you want it to do before you put it down on canvas. You say, "I want the nose to come forward." Make that action in midair first, then onto your canvas. Next you say, "I want this side plane of the nose to go back." Before putting that stroke on canvas, make it in midair. There should be a rhythm of application in every plane.

BALANCE
AND VARIETY

A rhythm of application doesn't only concern itself with making shapes recede and project, but also with variety and balance. Strokes all put down in the same direction become monotonous; they have to be broken with strokes in opposing directions. One stroke in one direction butted up against the next stroke in a somewhat opposite direction helps to make your painting ripple.

Robert Henri said, "Any stroke will not do." How right. One stroke applied with sensitivity and knowledge can become a piece of skin, another can be a tuft of hair, another a section of fabric. But strokes applied with little regard to this attitude of application can make those patches of paint just sit there saying and being nothing.

So balance and variety seem to be the key. I usually set the shape down with a stroke in a definite direction, then I affect it with a stroke opposite to it.

Although this book is about acrylic painting, a rhythm of application is utilized in *all* paintings and with *all* painting materials. It's your first step toward *painting a painting* regardless of the medium you're using.

TONE VALUES

Your palette's most important role—despite its array of colorful "puddles"—is to give you a chance to record the many tone values you see. Tone values—the lightness and darkness of your colors (and the most substantial element in painting a portrait)—are hard to identify because of their colored disguise. Beginners have difficulty with contrast of value because they refuse to relegate color to a secondary position in relation to tone. As a result, so many of their paintings are devoid of the dimension that tone values impart.

FIVE TONE
VALUES

What causes the tone values? Light travels in a straight line and its concentration on a round form causes contrasts that can be fit together like a five-piece jigsaw

A detail from my portrait of Dottie. Notice my rhythm of application; it's not applied carelessly.

A detail of Dottie's hair. The tones were painted with the brushstrokes moving in a direction opposite to the way the hair is combed.

Now the hair has been "combed" with paint. The tones have been stroked together in the same direction Dottie uses with her comb. When painting hair, put it in one way, and effect it the other.

Win Warren *Acrylic on canvas, 20" x 24".* I painted this at a portrait demonstration in Washington, D.C., in 1965. Painting in acrylic is a fascinating adventure. Each time I start a painting I can't rely on a former painting experience. When I work with oils I know what to expect, because oils always respond and act the same way. Acrylics are affected by climatic conditions, which make them react differently from day to day. You can see that I used very thick paint here. I don't know why it happened that way, but I'm glad. The model was very direct; the paint pictured the depth of his nature. Don't contrive a rhythm of application; let your manner of painting be an automatic response to the way the sitter affects you and your painting will emerge naturally.

puzzle. There are five basic tone values that dramatically add depth—the third dimension—to your two dimensional surface:

1. *Body (or general) tone:* the area or planes that are in line with the light source and are generally illuminated.

2. *Body shadow:* the area or planes of the subject that are darker because they're turned away from the straight rays of light.

3. *Cast shadows:* the dark tones that are caused by subjects standing in the path of the light source.

4. *Reflections:* tones caused by light striking surrounding areas and objects and bouncing back onto the subject.

5. *Highlights:* the planes in the general or body tone of the subject that are directly hit by the light.

Knowing that the five tone values exist is one thing, but putting them to use is another. These contrasts must make a tasteful, plausible image appear on the canvas. In order to do this, respect what the light is doing to your subject, and paint the five tone values with judgment. Let's now go over the five tone values in greater detail:

The *body tone* is a pattern of light value seen on all the planes toward the light. In portraiture, there's really only one body tone: it starts on the hair and travels down the face, neck, and clothing. It should have the same degree of illumination to maintain the solidity and oneness that is the subject. I venture to say there's hardly a body tone that doesn't have white in its admixture; white is the paint substitute for illumination.

The *body shadow* is made up of two parts: the edge of the shadow called a turning point (where the plane starts its turn away from the light), and the inside of the body shadow. The shape of the body shadow determines the inner drawing of the figure. No value or tone in the body shadow can be as light as the value of the body tone. The inner part of the body shadow often is affected by reflected light. It shouldn't be confused with reflection, which is mostly a matter of color (discussed later in this chapter). Often the turning edge of a shadow is darker than the whole of the shadow.

Cast shadows are caused by subjects standing in the way of the source of light. Their shapes are determined by what produces the shadow, where they fall, and how far or close they are from the light. Because they're a darker type of shadow, they can be a very designing element to the composition, and much discretion must be used to set them down. Sometimes an *illusion* of a cast shadow area would be better than painting exactly the shape and value you see. *All the values should work together for the picture, not for themselves.*

Reflections shouldn't be as light as the body tone, unless they're from another source of light, one purposely used for a special effect.

The *highlight* appears on any apex of a concave or convex plane that's in line with the light. It's the culmination of lightness on the body tone. As the body tone stands in line with the light, it gets lighter and lighter until it reaches out to be a highlight. Sometimes this is more a change of color than of value (I'll discuss this in greater depth later in this chapter). There are many highlights on a face; they not only inject added dimension but also impart the shiny look that's characteristic of skin texture.

Identify every value you see to be one of the five. Understand the function of each one; how each contributes a vital share to creating an illusion of depth.

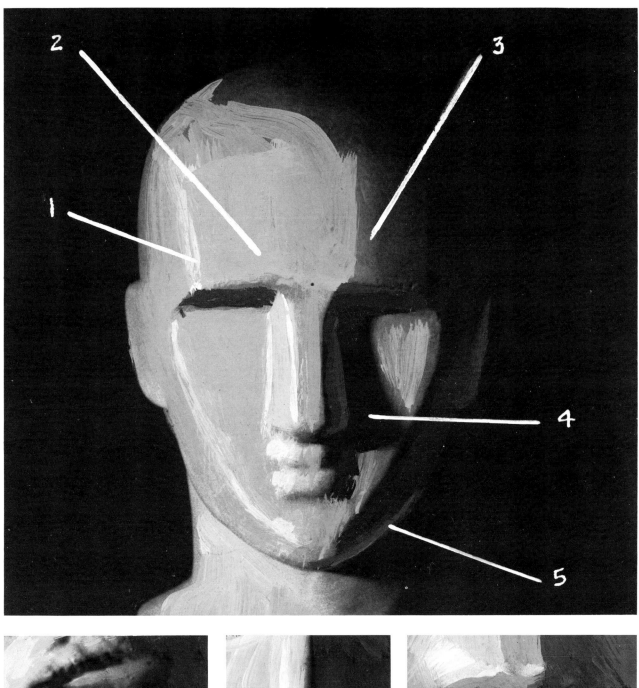

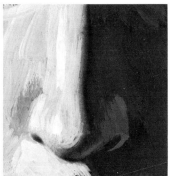

The five basic tone values are caused by one source of light. They serve to form the image. Painting a portrait is like painting a bowl of fruit rather than a single apple. Each feature, as well as the image, is made with the same five tone values. It's important to identify the tones you see. Only then can you make them function for your picture. Notice the tone values here: (1) highlight; (2) body tone; (3) body shadow; (4) cast shadow; (5) reflection. See if you can find the same tones on the eye, nose, and mouth pictured below.

Study of Indian Woman *Acrylic on canvas, 20" x 24".*
This painting was done on a canvas that was coated unevenly with gesso. The rough surface made me apply my
paint thickly to overtake the rhythm of the gesso coat.
I've identified the tone values in this painting to make you
more aware of them when you paint: (A) a cast shadow
of the figure, used only to fill the empty area of the
canvas, and help to balance the weight of the left side.
I took some license with the shadow, which was really
closer to the model; (B) a highlight area of the background to contrast strongly with the shadow side of the
figure; (C) body shadow area of the background, put in to
show that light was coming from the left, shining to the
right; (D) body tone of the image; (E) body shadow of
the image (all reflections in the shadow were eliminated
to understate the body in relation to the face); (F) body
tone of the face, accurately shaped in combination with an
accurate shape of the body shadow(G); (H) reflected light
on the neck of the model.

Study of Young Girl *Acrylic on canvas, 9" x 12"*. The little arrows point out cast shadows. Those shapes were first included in the over-all pattern of the body shadow, and later added with darker tone. The cast shadows are a little cooler in color than body shadows. Be ever so careful when you add them not to dig colorless holes in the face.

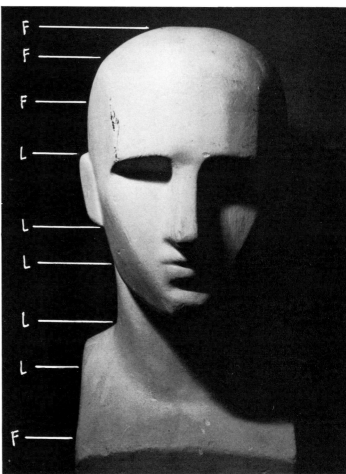

Russ *Acrylic on canvas, 16" x 20".* Sometimes we paint a pre-conceived idea rather than what we actually see. Instead of painting the value of the white in relation to the value of the skin, we paint what we think the teeth look like. Notice in this painting that the teeth are in the same value as the lightest tones of the face. This value is less than white. Compare it with the white square I painted in the corner to help you see values instead of teeth. If you have trouble seeing values, place a white index card on an easel next to your model, and compare the values on your subject to it.

Found-and-lost lines are visible upon close inspection. Lost lines (L) appear where a plane's outer shape meets another plane. These fuzzy parts of the periphery are very subtle, and can only be seen by comparing them to the more sharply defined contours.

The fourth and fifth components (rhythm of application and tone values) are put into use to fight the battle to create an illusion of depth on your flat canvas. There's still another weapon for this battle: *found-and-lost line*. Employing this component makes your subject live in a world of space.

I call this component found-and-lost line knowing full well that, in a dimensional rendering, edges result from two contrasting tones meeting each other. And while in painting *there's no such thing as a line*, I've discovered that my students understand this designation easier than the word *periphery*, a more accurate term.

The found-and-lost line is perhaps the most difficult maneuver in painting, because two unrelated colors and tones have to be fused together without making them look like a smudge. And in order to do this, brush dexterity becomes a factor. For a "lost" edge, pull the brush *away* from the canvas; start your stroke with *pressure* where you want a "found" line.

A three dimensional effect is quite a trick because you're trying to do on canvas what the model is doing in front of you—sitting in a sea of atmosphere. The tone values can certainly help to give this illusion of atmosphere, but they can't function if there's a sharp outline all around the head. This only gives the impression that the head's cut out and pasted onto the background.

You need found (sharp) and lost (fuzzy) lines to make the planes of the entire periphery project and recede. Bringing shapes forward and sending others back is a continuous maneuver that's based on a close observation of your model's outline, and on your understanding of the planes in his face. The edge has to be made up of many combinations of sharp and fuzzy strokes to give your model the appearance that he's sitting with space all around him. I find it's a good practice to paint the entire periphery in a fuzzy manner and then sharpen up the projecting edges.

Since you're going to have a so-called outline in your painting, you might as well do something about it. Don't let it be accidental; work with it for your picture's sake.

It's a paradox that although color is the most incidental of the painting components, it needs the most understanding. First, we must know the very nature of color, then we must learn how to use our paints as a physical substitute for nature's color. The phenomenon—a confusing one at that—is that light is our source of color, and it's made up of red, blue, and green. Furthermore, these three colors mix to make neutral lightness. All three colors shine all the time on everything to illuminate them. Sometimes this light is warm; sometimes it's cool. Skin color, for instance, doesn't look the same in the light of a snowy, wintry day as it does in a late afternoon sun.

We must make the colors of our palette do to the canvas what the light does to the subject. Paint can't be skin, hair, or clothing. It's tone above all, substance secondly, and color only finally that makes the transition from the actual to the pictorial possible. Color could surely be eliminated—and there are many media such as pen-and-ink, pencil, etc. that limit you to monochromatic rendering. However, as soon as we know that color is a possibility (and acrylic certainly has fantastic color opportunities), we'd feel the lack of it if it were missing. Although color only dramatizes and decorates the other more functional components, its importance can't be denied.

There are many helpful hints on color mixing throughout the book. You need a foundation to fully understand them. I hesitate to dictate rules to inhibit a student's choice of color composition, but I feel there are definite disciplines

I've removed all the lost lines from the periphery of this portrait to show how the absence of fuzzy edges can make the image appear to be pasted onto the background.

Here is the portrait as it really is. The role that found-and-lost lines plays to give you a feeling of dimension can't be ignored.

about nature's color that make color mixing logical and correct. Color mixing becomes easy if you know what colors you're seeing. They have to be defined so that you can translate them into paint. The artist can't just respond emotionally to color; he uses it, he has to make it *function*. So let's explain some truths of color which will help you choose the right ones for the right places.

PRIMARY COLORS AND THEIR COMPLEMENTS

Color is a word I use as a very general classification. All colors have three relative characteristics: *tone*—how light or dark it is in relation to its surroundings; *intensity*—how bright or dull it looks; and *hue*—how the color is tending. For instance, yellows have to be described as green yellows, true yellows, or orange yellows. And, of course, this is all relative. A reddish skin color mixture can turn orange if a violet type of red is painted near it. You must know what you're dealing with so you can dig into the color on your palette with conviction. The hue, tone, and intensity of the colors on my palette appear in Chapter 2.

The paint substitute for nature's primaries are red, blue, and yellow. When these primaries are mixed together, they make neutral darkness—black, or gray in lighter tones. A light ray has no substance; paint is *tone* as well as color.

The spectrum is made up of six colors: three warm, three cool. When two primaries are mixed, a secondary color results; it's the complementary color to the remaining primary color. Therefore, there are three secondary colors complementary to the three primary ones. The list below should help clarify this further.

WARM COLORS		COOL COLORS
primary yellow	complementary to	secondary violet
secondary orange	complementary to	primary blue
primary red	complementary to	secondary green

You'll notice that a color plus its complement contains the three primary colors.

There's also balance in color. You saw balance in the other components when you learned how light was balanced by dark; how one stroke was balanced by another, opposing one; how found lines were balanced by lost ones. In color, balance exists in the area of temperature. Cool colors have warm complements. Orange, the hottest color, has the coldest color, blue, as its complement; red, the coldest of the warm colors, has green, the warmest of the cool colors as its complement. Let's see how all this can dictate your use of color:

1. When mixed with each other, a color and its complement cancel each other's identity, and form a version of gray when white is added. This mixture is warm if more of the warm color is present; cool when more of the cool color is present.

2. A color finds its identity and is actually intensified if it's put in juxtaposition to its complement.

3. A color's intensity can be lessened, neutralized, or grayed by adding its complement.

4. Since a complement is used to gray a color, gray can then be considered a common complement to any color.

5. Where light *can* strike, color can appear in its full intensity (body tone).

6. Where the light *can't* strike, the color diminishes (the turning point of the body shadow and the edges of cast shadows). Color can be shadowed by adding a dark tone of the color's complement to the mixture, or this seemingly colorless gray can be painted with gray.

The chart on the opposite page shows my palette in action, the best way to explain how I use color. You'll notice that the arrangement here is geared to a right-handed person as opposed to the reproduction of my palette in Chapter 2. Since most of you will be working with the colors in this sequence, I felt it would have been confusing to picture my left-handed palette in this section on color. So here goes (reading from left to right): near the puddle of white are all the lightest tones of flesh color. They're very light pinks that even tend toward violet; they're the highlight mixtures. Near the warm colors—all those from cadmium yellow light to burnt sienna—are the general flesh colors. They're made by mixing any combination of a yellow and red into white. As you come to the middle of the palette, there are mixtures of slightly darker flesh that are seen just before the shadow (less white) and the cool gray tones that I use for the edge of the shadows. And near the darker warm colors are the darker flesh colors.

I painted a flesh-colored egg in the middle of the palette to show very basically where the colors go to achieve a feeling of solidity and illumination. It may not be proper to classify human heads as eggs, but all the problems of painting a head can be solved more simply by painting an egg. The flesh colors on the left side of the egg are all the mixtures you see on the left of the palette. These colors are lightened by the highlights which are the cooler, more reddish or violetish colors. Then, as the egg falls into shadow, there are darker flesh colors that blend into a line of gray—that's the turning point, mixtures of black and white plus a cool color—any violet, blue, or green. This gray color is used to paint in the entire shape of the shadow. On the egg this shape is easy compared to how it falls on the forehead, eyes, nose, mouth, and chin. Gray turns color into shadow because where light doesn't strike color can't show. Beyond the edge of the shadow, the general illumination of the room bounces some reflected light into the shadow, causing color to appear. This is where shadowed flesh color is used. Illuminated flesh is warm color into white; shadowed flesh can be mixed by putting color into darkened white, which is gray. My shadowed flesh is never as light as the body tone. This shadowing of a color can also be done by taking a complement (green, violet, or blue) and mixing it into a dark flesh mixture, one with less white. Many students think they just have to take green, violet, or blue and put it into their flesh colors to get the shadow. This mixture can be chalky because there's really too much white in basic flesh mixture to evolve it into shadow. You'll notice a cast shadow on the neck of the egg. This darker type of shadow is treated the same way. It has an edge, which is cool, and a warm colored interior. On the far right of the palette are some mixtures of dark colors. These are accent colors used where you see the darker darks of the eyes, nose, and mouth. You have to look at these colors, and see how they look to you. That's really the root of getting the right color. If you can see it, you can mix it.

I use the same arrangement for my oil palette as I do for acrylics and when I paint still life as well as portraits. I simplify the palette when I paint outdoors. I don't use as many colors, and use other colors when the need arises. For instance, when I paint flowers I use all the violets and reds I can find. If I have to paint an unusual costuming, I may use other colors. So even though I may add and subtract, there are two that I can't live without—black and white; they give me a wide range of values, and this to me is much more important than color. The palette itself is a medium gray, giving me a neutral place to mix my colors.

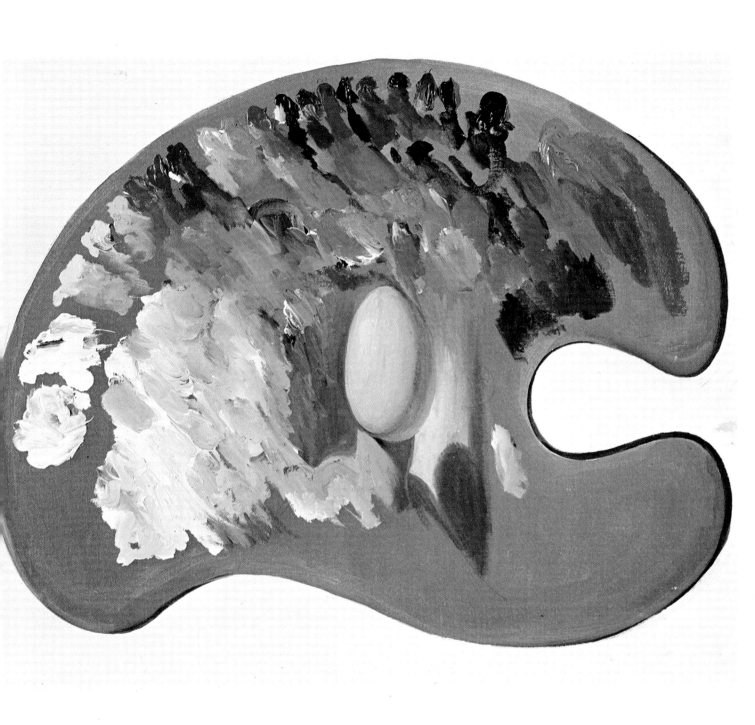

7. The highlight is where the light strikes so hard that the color disappears in the glaring illumination. The color of this light is relatively complementary to the color it's on. The highlight on skin is sometimes just cooler flesh rather than a lighter tone.

8. Since a body shadow is affected by reflected light, there's color in the shadow. But it's diminished color in relation to the body tone. This can be color, toned down with gray or with its complement.

9. A reflection is a conditional color; it depends on the conditions that cause it.

10. When your colors are complemented properly, your painting gets the luminous, vibrant look that's the very nature of light.

COLOR MIXTURES FOR BACKGROUNDS

Color is very relative. Colors react to each other, thus there can be no formula mixtures. There are, however, some logical generalities that can aim your mixtures in the right direction.

When in doubt about background colors, use gray, warm or cool. When you want your background a color, make sure it's toned down in intensity so it can perform as a background—something that's far away.

COLOR MIXTURES FOR HAIR

All hair is a version of yellow—from light blondes to dark browns and brunettes. For blondes: yellow-green, any of the yellows, plus white where the light strikes; in the shadows, gray-violet (black, white, and Thalo crimson) to throw the color into shadow; then darker yellows inside the shadow. For brunettes: same as blonde, only less white. Since the color is more orange, you have to swim in burnt umber and burnt sienna. Blue can be used to "shadowize" the basic color. Highlights on hair are gray-blue or gray-violet. Hair also gets glints of reflections of lighter, brighter versions of its body tone. Black hair isn't black, but a very diminished yellow, burnt umber, and dark gray with blue violet shadows.

COLOR MIXTURES FOR SKIN

Skin must have white as a base because it's seen where the light strikes. Into white add a yellow and a red and try for a general tone—one that will accommodate and accept lighter and lighter tones that end up with a highlight. Thalo crimson, cadmium yellow, and white make a good highlight color. The student generally makes the mistake of starting his flesh tone too light. He should start in the area just before the turning point. After all, the shadow color never gets near the beginning of that build-up of lights toward the highlight.

COLOR MIXTURES FOR SHADOW FLESH

For shadows in the flesh areas, use grayed darker flesh colors mixed into a puddle of gray (black and white, some yellow ochre, and red oxide). Or put a bit more yellow ochre and red oxide into your flesh mixture to reduce the properties of white and add a touch of blue, green, or violet.

CLOTHING

Make sure you relate the illumination on the color of the clothing to the amount of illumination on the face. Don't paint any color without thinking of the degree of lighting or the degree of shade.

In these last two chapters, we've covered the seven components. You'll see in the demonstration chapters that follow how each and every component is utilized no matter what style or technique I use.

Chapter 6

Painting Techniques

This chapter will serve as the bridge over the gulf that separates the theoretical part of painting—my seven components—from the practical part—the sixteen demonstrations to follow. With each component, I was able to give you bits of information to benefit your painting experience. Those hints, though, were entirely within the context of the particular subject. And in my demonstrations, I illustrate how paint was used for each specific problem. This bridging chapter, then, is necessary to inject some thoughts about certain techniques that I use in *all* my paintings. I hope you'll put them to use during your excursions through "portrait painting land." You'll find them a preview for the many demonstrations to come.

Just as the pianist must strike the keys no matter what melody he plays, and just as a carpenter must hammer his nails no matter what structure he builds, the painter has to apply his paint no matter what he paints. Even though all pianists use the same piano keys, all carpenters use the same tools, and all painters use the same implements, all of them do their jobs with a personal touch. I apply my paint in certain manners, and the following illustrates my techniques: (1) Progression of applications; (2) Working from the top down; (3) Painting backgrounds. Now, let's take them one by one.

PROGRESSION OF APPLICATIONS

To illustrate this procedure, I used the teeth area of my portrait of Russ. The mouth is the only feature in the face that moves so radically, strongly influencing the entire area around it. Sargent said, "A portrait is a picture of a person with something wrong with his mouth." How true. And the most difficult expression of the mouth is the smile, especially when teeth are showing. This has to look spontaneous, and the way the paint is handled to depict this area will strongly dictate its attitude.

First, I paint a tone to represent the teeth (which are farthest back) with a stroke that covers a larger area on the canvas than the teeth actually do on the face. I usually paint from back to front, the same way I view my subject matter (like painting eyes before I paint the glasses). And I make the first shape larger than it really is so that the next shape of a different value can cut into it and shape it in.

Next, I cut down the teeth area with the values of the lips. Finally, I add lighter and darker tones to accentuate the dimension and define the expression.

WORKING FROM THE TOP DOWN

Working from the top down is another technique I always use. I explain its application to a portrait by using a sliced loaf of bread as an analogy. I tell my students, "Pretend you're painting a sliced loaf that's standing up on end. You'll have to paint one slice at a time, and in order to do this you'll have to work from the top down." Doing it this way, you can correct the underside of one stroke

Paint the teeth area larger than it actually is.

Cut into the teeth area with the lips in another value.

Add lights and darks for dimension and expression.

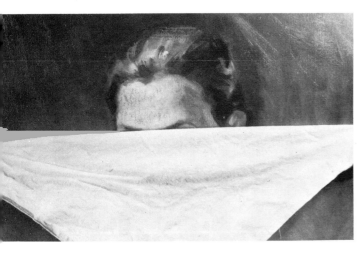

The cloth limits your work to the forehead area.

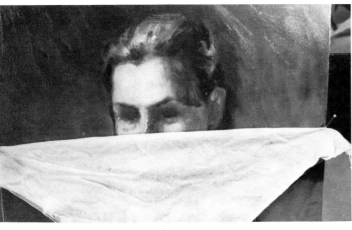

Notice the difference between the forehead and the new, undone area that's been unmasked by the cloth.

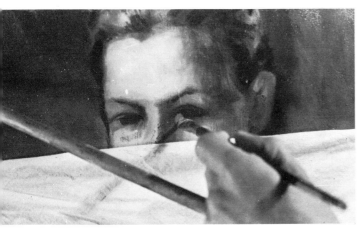

Lighter lights being worked into the eye area.

Now the body tone of the cheeks have been lightened.

The paint is laid in near the figure, cutting into its periphery.

The shadow color is painted in broad, horizontal strokes.

Vertical strokes are used to join the shadow tone with the tone of the first step.

Using a big brush, these vertical strokes are blended with horizontal strokes.

(a slice) with the top of the next stroke (the next slice).

Let's now apply this to a portrait. After boldly laying in a light and dark pattern to represent the body tone and body shadow of the face, situating the larger masses of the head, I then repaint with more care. To do this, I observe and paint each area one at a time, starting at the forehead and working down.

A good exercise to get you into the swing of painting from the top down is to pin a cloth across your picture to limit your work to one area—the forehead first. After adding lighter tones to the body tone, and darkening the shadow, lower the cloth to the next general area—below the eyes. Again, add lighter lights and darker darks to this area before lowering the cloth to the next position on the canvas, and so on until the entire face is brought up to the same stage of development. Eventually, you'll be able to do this mentally, but until you can, using the cloth will impose a much needed discipline. Your individual stroke should also be handled in this manner, from the top down. It's only the top of your stroke that counts; the bottom of it will be corrected by the top of your next stroke.

PAINTING BACKGROUNDS

Since backgrounds are a personal matter of taste, I can't help you choose the colors for them. But there's a method that I use to make my backgrounds look atmospheric, and it can improve any background you'll put into your paintings. Keep in mind that the background doesn't only represent the portion directly in back of your model, it also has to function as the model's entire environment. Your background should be just that: a large area of space in which your model lives and has room to breathe.

I often make the tone of the background dark where it nears the source of light. For instance, if the light is coming from above, I make the top area of the background darker then the bottom area. If the light source is from the left, I grade the values of the background from dark on the left to light on the right. This shows where the light is striking.

Just as I use tone values to help me with my backgrounds, I also use modulations of warm and cool colors. Even if I paint a background all of one tone, the tone is made up of a warm and cool color. One way I effect this is to paint a cool color and glaze a warm color over it. Another way is to mix them together.

I always start my backgrounds around the figure, working out to the edge of the canvas. The background can't be just filled in if it's going to look like the space the model sits in. It has to be painted with brushstrokes of atmosphere.

Rather than describe how the background of each portrait in this book was painted, here's a good basic, general procedure that can apply to all portraits.

I mix up a large amount of the color I want the background to be, and paint it in, cutting into the figure. While it's still wet, I correct the outline by working it over the background color. I lay in this color with strokes not much longer than 2″. As I fill in the canvas toward where I want it darker, I use a little darker version of the color.

I spread this color out further than I want it so that I can put my next tone on it. This next tone is a shadow version of the color made by adding the color's complement. It's laid in in a shape I want the darker area. I blend this value into the existing one with a series of opposing strokes that resemble teeth. Then, with a blender, or any large, soft brush, I fuse these teeth with strokes opposite to them. With a darker tone of the color of the background, I continue painting out to the edges of the canvas, blending in the same manner as just described.

Study the demonstrations that follow; see how these painting techniques were incorporated into each painting. Naturally, you won't be able to see my procedure of working from top to bottom; you'll just have to take my word for it.

Demonstrations

Demonstration 1   A Character Study

I know this gentleman well, he's Bob Benham, a fellow painter here on Cape Ann, Massachusetts. I've found that painters make excellent models. They have an insight about posing for portraits; I guess they sympathize with their colleagues struggling behind their easels with a creative challenge. I was intrigued with his appearance, because the flashy quality of his white hair and ruddy complexion contrasted so strongly with his calm, gentle way and his good nature.

It's hard to put the motivation element of a painting into words; it's such a personal attitude, a personal reaction to a sense of sight. I see something and it calls out to me; it seeks expression. As soon as I face the easel and begin to paint, I can describe the painting process more easily, because it's a practical rather than a theoretical process taking place.

ESTABLISHING THE SHADOW PATTERN

My first job was to situate the head on the canvas in the position I wanted it. I made some marks, what I call scaffolding, to enable me to put my paint down in the right place. I made bold marks to indicate the top and the bottom of the portrait area; this was the size limitation of the head in relation to the size of the canvas. I didn't want to get involved in an intricate composition, I simply wanted head and shoulders; I just wanted a character study.

These initial marks were done with black thinned with water. I wiped my brush so that I could just drag it over the surface. Then I made some marks to indicate the front plane of the face in relation to the side planes. Other marks followed, to delineate the proportions of the face: where the eyebrows were; where the eyeline was (to locate the eye pits); the end of the nose; the mouth and the shadow under the lower lip. The chin mark was already there when I had decided how big to make the head. These marks were followed by some angular lines in relation to the head to suggest the body. This is all I have to do with lines before I begin a painting. I'm not making a drawing that I'll color; the lines are, as I said earlier, simply scaffolding for me to stand on as I make my picture out of paint.

THE DRAWING

Actually, whenever I start on a white or toned down canvas, I take a dark tone of gray and paint in the shape of the shadow. This shadow starts at the top of the head and doesn't stop until it gets to the bottom of the canvas, or as far down as I want to go. It's one continuous shape; it helps to give a feeling of solidity to the head.

Since the light came from the left, the shadow started at the right side of the hair. Then it cut into the hairline, traveled down the two sections of the forehead (the upper part and the eyebrow section). Because the light came from above, it blacked out the eye sockets. The whole right side of the face was in shadow. There was a cast shadow from the nose that was added to the shadow on that side. The shadow traveled onto the upper lip area (where the mustache grows), the upper lip, on the right side of the lower lip, and onto the chin. A little bit of light hit the chin, and a couple of little shadows were put in to indicate the ears. I didn't want to get too involved with the ear at this stage; I just wanted to get it in the right place in relation to the eyes and the mouth.

The whole cast shadow on the neck from the head was one mass shadow that I suggested in one value. By reducing it down to one tone, I found it easier to get a good shape out of that shadow. Don't think of putting in all the values of the shadow. As soon as you do this, you lose sight of the entire shape. And the shape is more important than all the intricate values the over-all shadow contains.

The background was put in dark on the left side to help show that the light was coming from the left, and to make the so-called line at the right side of the face. This shadow pattern was done with black and white plus a little umber to make a warm gray. The paint was loosened with water to ease the application.

MODELING LIGHT AND DARK

At this stage, there was a big change from what I had done just previously. The whole light side, or the illuminated area of the face, was made darker. This was because it was filled in with the local color of each area: the local color of the hair, forehead, nose, cheek, mouth area, and chin. Naturally, color will darken a value, but laying in this area of the light side should be darker than many people think. It's not the beautiful bloom on skin; it's a basic tone. You might say it's an investment you're making to be able to add those beautiful blooming colors onto.

Because I had shaped the shadow, I was able to put in the shape of the light side, or wherever the light struck in the colors that I saw. Naturally, all my colors included white, because I was working on the illuminated plane, and white illuminates all color. But I never saturate a color with so much white that I get it chalky; I take the rawness out of the color by presenting it as the projecting plane.

I created a soft edge between the light and dark areas by overlapping the light side with the shadow area, then used the shadow gray again trying to fuse the two tones together. This was done on each section: the forehead, the nose, the eyes, the mouth, the chin. When you're working with fast-drying acrylics you can't say, "I'll blend it later."

THE BACKGROUND

After modeling the light and dark sides together, I decided to paint the background dark on the right side of the face. Now I had an entire dark background, a medium-toned shadow, and a light area. As I painted the picture, I saw Bob against a dark background, and it's much easier to relate your values if you paint the situation that you see. This is important in portraiture. Make sure you organize your studio, your drape or atmosphere in back of the figure, to be a nice tonal environment for your model.

DEVELOPING THE LIGHT AREAS

I developed this portrait sketch further by adding lighter lights to the planes toward the light. The hair seemed lighter because I wanted the hair to come out. The darker little tones in the hair were the lights I put in earlier. Now they've become the shadows, but they're not as dark as the shadow pattern I had established earlier.

There was a lighter area in the upper part of the head; these were the lighter tones I added to the basic forehead section. Those little lighter tones hitting the upper part, the top planes of the eyebrows, made those features stand out. The way to make something stand out is with lighter lights, not with darks. But lighter lights are only possible when you start dark enough.

**GLAZING
THE SHADOW**

The whole light plane that was the solidity before was now more fleshy because lighter tones are added on any concave or convex plane. The development of the shadow area was more complex. The shadow until now was still the warm gray I had started with. It appeared cooler because of all the warm flesh colors. Some reflected light had to be added into the shadow to prevent it from looking so flat. I mixed yellow ochre, red oxide, and a breath of white with gel, and glazed this color onto the shadow. This procedure can be frightening, because the gel mixture is milky and makes the entire shadow area look like it'll be covered with this film. It dries clear, however, and this is why the experiments in the front of the book are so important. Doing a portrait is no time to get acquainted with the idiosyncracies of a strange medium.

This glaze dried quickly. Then I added the darker darks for the irises of the eyes, the cast shadow of the nose, eye socket area, the creases caused by the mouth's constant movements, and the darks where the head cast a shadow on the body and defined the features in shadow.

I added some reflected light into the shadow area because a reflection is a legitimate tone value that completes the illusion of a third dimension. As the rightmost edge of the face met the background, there were a few lighter values where the general illumination of the room bounced back on those planes catching just a little light. Be careful not to make reflections too light.

**FINAL
SITTING**

The last sitting for me just seems to be a matter of correcting little areas. I tried to develop the little intricacies of the lightest light planes that were already boldly stated, and I tried to soften the darkest dark shadow patterns that I socked in earlier. These had been statements much like those in a telegram. Now I had to write a novel. The picture had to stand up under closer and longer observation than just a surface likeness. It needed little points of accuracy. Naturally, the over-all likeness started from the very first; that's the whole attitude. But then, when it came to closer observation, there were little things about the mouth, about the nose, and the eyes that can be put into the basic "all rightness" of the entire head. It was at this point that I thought it would be more characteristic to show a turtleneck shirt under the overshirt, and I wanted to leave it very sketchy.

**COLOR
MIXTURES**

Now to help you out about the various color mixtures: There was a warm light striking the subject, so all the areas that were illuminated were warm colors. The shadow pattern was rather dark and quite gray. My basic flesh mixture that accommodated all my lighter light additions was composed of red oxide, raw sienna, cadmium red light, and white. Where it seemed to dull down and mute a little bit more toward shadow, I added burnt umber and Thalo yellow green.

The development of the lighter light areas were a brighter mixture of flesh. Instead of using red oxide, raw sienna, and white, I used cadmium red light, yellow ochre, and white. I just upped the octave, made it more intense, because I wanted the light to strike intensely. As I reached out for those highlights (this is where the glaring light usually kills the colors so much), instead of getting more intense I made the color less intense. I didn't go into duller flesh tones, but reached out for a relative complement to flesh to make somewhat of a shine. I used Thalo crimson, yellow ochre, and white. Thalo crimson is on the violet side and thus turned my flesh color cooler.

The highlights on the hair (basically burnt umber and white on the light side, lightened with yellow ochre and white) at this point were made flashingly light by using white, a touch of black and blue. An extremely cool color on that warm foundation, and this cool and warm working together gives the fullness of life.

Complements fill in a deficiency. If any area lacks dimension or lacks light, it's because there's a lacking color. When you're working with yellow, for example, the lacking color is the mixture of the other two primaries. So violet has to be incorporated. But to do this successfully you have to do away with your pre-conceived ideas of what colors look like. The violet I'm referring to isn't the color of a violet flower in springtime; it's the violet in the spectrum that can be as light as white and as dark as black. So the highlights on this portrait are "violetish": white, Thalo crimson (a little more towards the red), toned down with yellow ochre (its complement) to prevent the violet from being too harsh.

Step 1 I made some marks to enable me to put my paint down in the right place. I call these compositional hieroglyphics my scaffolding.

Demonstration 1: A Character Study 91

Step 2 This step has nothing to do with color, because the shadow side was painted in gray and the light area was the tone of the canvas. My shadow pattern runs the entire length of the image, from the top of the head to the clothing.

Step 3 At this stage, I introduced color into the face. But the flesh tone I used was a basic one that would give me the opportunity to go lighter. It was the investment I had to make to get a beautiful, blooming flesh color.

Demonstration 1: A Character Study　93

Step 4 (Above) Now I started to add more light to my light side and more dark to my dark side. The development of the shadow was more complex; the warm flesh colors made it appear cooler. With a mixture of yellow ochre, red oxide, gel, and a touch of white I glazed over the shadow.

Step 5 (Right) For me, the last sitting always seems to constitute correction of little areas. There were small highlighted areas to paint in; there were little dark accents that had to be added. Work around the eyes, nose, and mouth polished the picture further, adding to the over-all likeness. Then I decided to paint Bob in a turtleneck shirt under his overshirt. I felt it was more characteristic of him.

Demonstration 2 A Larger Composition

Painting a large composition can be compared to putting in time-and-a-half on a job. This is because there's so much work that *has* to be done—and *can* be done —between sittings. By and large, with head-and-shoulder compositions, I work only when my model is with me.

My canvas for this full figure portrait was heavily textured for two reasons. First, because the strength of the canvas would be able to withstand the large expanse. Secondly, the rough texture would make it easier for me to paint soft, fuzzy edges, the effect I wanted for this painting.

I call this Don Rodrigo because of the Mexican chair the model's sitting on, and his Mexican mustache. In reality, the model is Herb Rogoff, without whose help this book could never have been possible.

Step 1 This diagram shows how I use the size of the head as a point of measurement. Line 1 was set down as the place for the top of the chair. Line 2 was where the top of the head would be, and line 3 was where I wanted the seat of the chair. Now that I had a size for the entire figure, I could break it up into fractions. The head was less than one third of the figure, and the width was a little less than three heads.

Step 2 As soon as I found the size and place for the head, I sketched the sizes of the other shapes of the image.

Step 3 I began painting this large composition by doing the head in the same way I always work. This is how the painting looked after the first sitting.

Step 4 Before he posed again, I painted the background and the chair, and massed in a dark tone for the body. I related these values to the already painted face. During the second sitting, I developed the face almost to completion, and put in a value to locate the hands. Even though the face constitutes such a small percentage of the canvas, it still must be the focal point. I felt I had to paint the face first, then relate the rest of the canvas to it. Notice that the hands are in a darker key of values than the face, which reduces their importance in the painting.

Step 5 (Above) I worked on the portrait again between sittings. I repainted the background, cutting into the outline of the figure, and developed the chair a little more. During this sitting, I reshaped the periphery, and added the shadows to the figure. This forced me to get the correct outline of the hands.

Step 6 (Right) The finished picture. To finish, I added more light to the illuminated areas and developed the hands with more contrast.

A Portrait Demonstration

This painting was done at a demonstration for the Rockport Art Association in 1969. Dana is a teen-ager who lives on my street. He is good-looking in a very interesting way, and since I had painted him before, I knew him to be an excellent model. A painting demonstration is a double challenge: completing a painting and holding the attention of an audience. With this task before me, I needed someone like Dana.

THE SUPPORT

I chose to start on a toned Masonite panel. Its gray-green color, typical of pastel paper, and its somewhat smooth, absorbent surface, produced a pastel-like quality in the painting. Acrylic is a chameleon, it changes its character according to its environment. A definition of intelligence is the ability to adjust to any given environment. I'm not saying acrylics are intelligent; they're just adaptable to any idea on the part of the painter. The artist must be clever about his materials.

The Masonite was prepared with a coat of gesso to seal the smooth surface. In the second coat of gesso, I mixed chromium oxide green and burnt sienna to make a ground of neutral color and value, which is easy to work on.

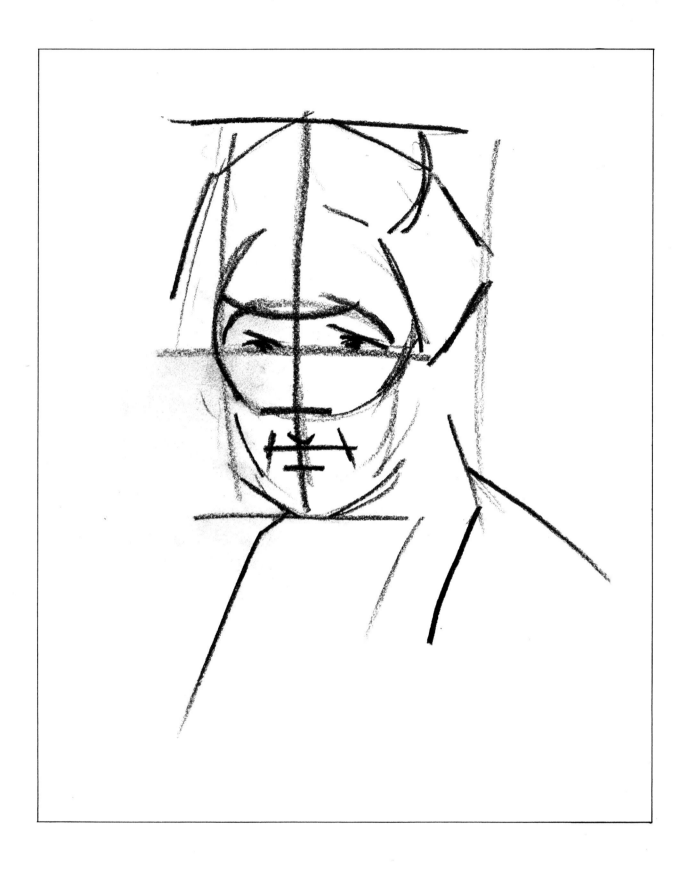

Step 1 Composition and drawing. My first considerations were how large I wanted the head to be in relation to my canvas, and where it should be situated on the canvas. Then I began the drawing.

Step 2 Here, a dark tone blots out all the areas where the light couldn't strike. Notice, on the right, how a dark background tone, instead of a line, was used to show the shape of the image. A mixture of white, cadmium red light, raw sienna, and a little burnt umber (in a tone slightly darker than basic flesh) was painted along the turning point.

Step 3 The flesh tone was painted and worked into that color along the turning point. Don't be afraid to cut a background into the shape of the image. It gives you the chance to shape it again with more care; it makes the background look like it's behind the image.

Step 4 (Above) Color was added into the shadow with a mixture of red oxide, raw sienna, a little white, and gel. Darker tones were added into the shadow (Thalo crimson, burnt umber, and a little Thalo blue). The outer shape was painted; notice the found-and-lost lines.

Step 5 (Right) The light side of the face was developed with the many little changes of color. Then the highlight pattern was added. Except for a little gel used in the shadow, water was the only medium I used with my color.

2 HOUR DEMO

Demonstration 4 Oil Glaze Over Monochrome

Janice Pozzi is a charming, ingenuous young lady, warm and very open in her ways. This prompted me to do a full face picture of her, fully aware that this is a tricky view for a painter. You see, everyone's face has two *different sides*, and although you may not notice this when you look at the person, these naturally uneven sides can make a portrait look as if the artist made a mistake. Turning the model's head away from full face, however slight that movement may be, will prevent the two sides from ever being viewed symmetrically. Despite all this, though, I like the full face pose; it looks natural and honest. The portrait of my brother in an earlier chapter cried out to be painted full face because he's so direct. I don't see how I could have painted him in any other pose. And, as I said, this is how Janice's countenance affected me as well.

COMBINING OIL AND ACRYLICS

Even though a large portion of Janice's portrait was done with acrylics, it must be considered an oil painting because my last layer of application was painted with oil colors. This should answer all those questions about the right way to classify pictures painted with more than one medium. The paintings of the past, painted over underpaintings of a different medium, are legitimately classed as oil paintings.

This brings us to a controversy that seems to be brewing about the use of oil colors over acrylics. Despite the constant assurance provided by the manufacturers of art materials, some experts now claim that the oil film, being more brittle, will flake off when the flexible acrylic underpainting begins to move as a result of atmospheric conditions, jostling, etc. We know that for many years before the inception of acrylics, oil colors were painted over material that cracked, and the oil paint cracked with it. An oil painting is constructed of many layers, placed one on top of the other, and if these layers become complicated or are not applied with care, the picture stands a good chance of deteriorating. I feel that acrylics have not only performed a great service for the artist but for oil paintings as well, because acrylics make the oil application simpler.

So I really don't concern myself with these arguments. A lifetime isn't long enough for me to paint all the pictures I want to; I can't take the time to get involved in hypothetics. I do, however, take great care that my acrylic underpaintings are prepared properly to accept my oil applications. To do this, I use only water with my acrylics, which helps to create texture much like that of a blackboard. Oil paint won't adhere well to glossy surfaces, something you should keep in mind when you use an acrylic underpainting for oil applications.

THE DRAWING

As in my other demonstrations, I started with the placement and general proportioning so I could aim my paint in the right places. I decided to use a dark-toned canvas, because Janice's alabaster-like complexion and blonde hair provoked this kind of approach.

I sketched Janice's head with white chalk, a medium I find I use more frequently with acrylics; I can wipe the construction lines away with a damp cloth or paint right over them without contaminating my color. The chalk marks direct me to the darks of the underplanes of the features and to the shadow cast on the hair from the face. These will be my darkest darks.

THE UNDERPAINTING

The illuminated planes were carefully painted so they'd need no correction with the background tone—a very hard tone to match up. The whole shadow pattern was set down in the same tone as the background.

The entire underpainting was done monochromatically in tones of violet. I used a mixture of Mars violet, Thalo blue, burnt umber, and some white to tone the canvas. I used this same mixture—with varying amounts of white—for all my values. At this point, I found I had to begin blending my tones. A pointer to keep in mind about fusing two tones is not to try to blend two extreme values together.

The pattern of the light area was painted in a gray just a few degrees lighter than the tone of the canvas. This tone makes an easy adjustment to the surface it's applied to. Then I lightened the entire illuminated plane, taking care not to go too near to the shadow pattern with this stronger contrast. This gradual buildup of lighter tones on the light planes, with each one getting progressively smaller, led me to the next step.

PUTTING IN THE HIGHLIGHTS

M. A. Rasko, the fine painter I studied with, used to say, "Helen, make it, break it, and make it again." He voiced this advice with regard to oil painting, but it certainly applies to acrylics also. My highlights in Step 2 are more obvious than on the finished underpainting in Step 4. That's because they underwent Rasko's "make it, break it, make it again."

First, the shapes of the highlights had to be painted in to define the shapes within the light areas. They're definite important tonal elements. In order to shape the highlights, you must blend, but blending isn't a tone value, it's a process you must use to get a soft effect. To soften the highlight into the general tone, take a brush wetted with water, and break down the harshness of the edges of the highlights where they meet the body tone. Since this can often soften the highlight too much, or even almost remove it, this will give you the chance to put the highlight on again. Remember, "make it, break it, make it again."

GLAZING THE UNDERPAINTING

Putting glazes of color over an underpainting may seem easy, but I've always approached this procedure with great care. Using acrylics for an underpainting, however, has managed to relieve some of my apprehension, because if things don't go right, the oil glazes can be removed with turpentine without damaging the underpainting.

To glaze Janice's portrait, I carefully set up my colors on a white palette, which I use only for this technique of painting. Since I'd be working transparently, the white palette gives me a chance to see how strong or weak the glazes would be.

I made sure I had very soft and very clean brushes. A glaze of color is so tender and delicate that even a slightly dirty brush can contaminate the color and ruin the application. Although it may seem silly to stress the importance of rags at this point, I'm very fussy about them—especially when I'm glazing. I've found that I can more successfully glaze when I first apply too much intensity of color and then wipe it down to its proper color with a rag. Turkish toweling—cut in 4″ squares—is ideal.

As a thinner for my glaze, I used a mixture of linseed oil, damar varnish, and turpentine, equal parts of each. This proportion is important, because too much of one ingredient can make your glaze either too oily or too flaky. There are commercially prepared oil painting mediums on the market that are formulated for this purpose.

Cadmium red light and yellow ochre were used for the flesh area—in admixture, of course. Into this general color I carefully worked in some local color—to the cheeks, lips, and shadows. I used a glaze of Chinese vermilion for the clothing, and a warm green for the background. Raw sienna was glazed over the hair.

Sometimes a freshly glazed picture has a harshness of color and seems too luminous. This luminosity, in time, softens to a grand glow. As I said, this method seems easy, but don't expect too much from your first attempts. Everyone must experience and experiment in order to personally see the effects of a procedure. There's a limit to what you can gain from personal instruction and the written page.

Step 1 I used a dark-toned canvas because of the smooth, young girl complexion of my model. The construction lines of her head were sketched with white chalk, which is easily removed with damp rag, or covered with paint.

Step 2 I carefully painted the illuminated planes. If they had needed correction, it would have been difficult, because I would have had to match the ground color.

Step 3 The highlights were set in to define the shapes in
the lighted areas. But after they had served this important
but temporary function, the highlights would have to be
broken down.

Step 4 (Above) My underpainting was completed—all in values of violet. It was ready for oil glazes. It's at this point that you appreciate the fast-drying properties of acrylic; an underpainting has to be completely dry, and underpaintings prepared even with fast-drying oil colors have to wait a few days until they're ready to be glazed with oils.

Step 5 (Right) I thinned my oil colors with a painting medium composed of turpentine, linseed oil, and damar varnish. You can make this yourself, or you can buy the many brands on the market. I used a soft, very clean brush to glaze my colors over the acrylic underpainting.

Demonstration 5 Acrylic Glaze Over Monochromatic Impasto

When I met this man and was to do his portrait, I felt I wanted to do it in a craggy way. This ranch owner in New Mexico affected me this way, just like those virile cowboys in the cigarette commercials. I wanted my rhythm of application to do a lot of talking for me. But I realized that acrylic isn't the kind of material you can lay on heavily without first going into a great deal of preparation.

LAYING IN THE IMPASTO

To work as heavily as I wanted for my "outdoorsy" look, I would have to pre-mix modeling paste into every color. Using modeling paste with color in this manner, however, while giving it thickness, wouldn't at the same time offer me a chance to get a fluid, juicy quality. The thickness I wanted would also be too cumbersome to work with, so I approached it in this fashion:

I mixed modeling paste into white, and with a palette knife I put a layer of this mixture (about $1/16''$ thick) over the entire canvas. While it was still wet, I used a bristle brush to paint into it with more of a white mixture. You might say I was sculpting with paint. To simplify the job and to give me a chance to later develop color with glazes, I dissolved all color and value out of my application. I was able to see the pattern of brushstrokes in the thick, colorless substance by situating a spotlight off to one side of my canvas.

I then put in a slight bit of gray to define the shadow on the nose, the shadow caused by the smile, the shadow on the side plane of the face, and some shadow on the hat. I let it all dry.

GLAZING THE COLORS

Now it was time for me to glaze my color over the thick application. I mixed some gloss medium with equal parts of water, and used this to thin the color (burnt sienna) enough to glaze the face. A little heavier amount of burnt sienna with some cadmium red light was used for the cheek; for the nose, I added some Thalo crimson into the mixture. I let that application dry, and then put another glaze over the shadow to make it look more colorful.

A mixture of Thalo blue and burnt umber was used on the hair; the hat was glazed with raw sienna, with some burnt umber and thio violet into the shadow side; and I glazed Thalo blue over the shirt.

I had to paint the background opaquely to get it as dark as I wanted. There are also some opaque passages on the hat; they're just corrections, and I'm sorry I had to do them, but I often have to sacrifice my handling of the paint for the sake of the over-all composition and design.

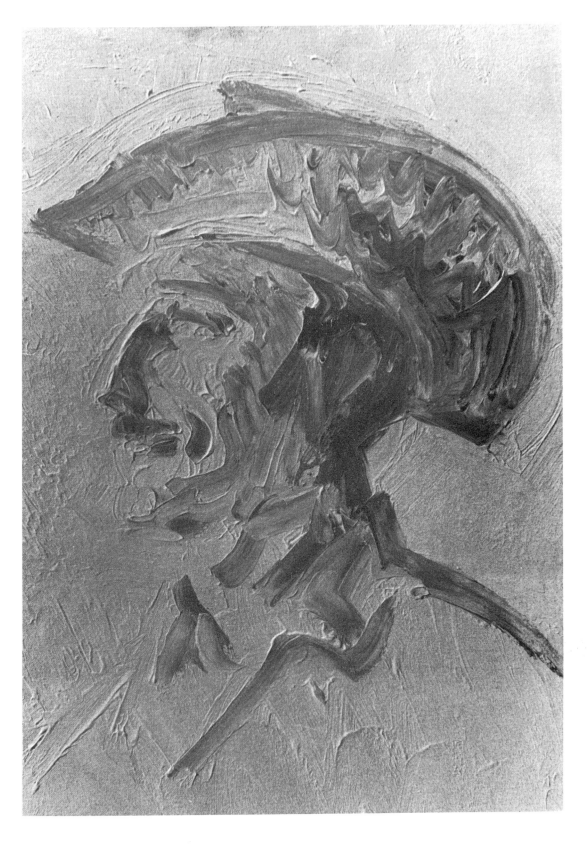

Step 1 After covering the entire canvas with a thin layer of modeling paste mixed into white, I painted into the wet substance with a bristle brush, adding gray to define all the shadows. I now had a monochromatic impasto underpainting that I could glaze as soon as it was dry.

Demonstration 5: Acrylic Glaze Over Monochromatic Impasto 117

Step 2 (Above) The initial glazes. Because acrylic color applications dry waterproof, subsequent glazes can't move or smear the existing glazes. A monochromatic underpainting should be in a very light key of values to withstand the darkening that glazes of color cause.

Step 3 (Right) The finished picture. My second application of glazes added more luster to the shadow areas. The background was painted with opaque color; that's the only way I was able to get it as dark as I wanted it to be.

Demonstration 6   Using Limited Tone

The model motivates the paint interpretation. This lovely Japanese woman reminded me of oriental culture and oriental art, and this influenced my painting. You'll notice that the background is a plain, flat color. The clothing, the hair, and the face were also handled with values simpler than I ordinarily use on my other portraits. I did this because it's an oriental attitude to respect the flatness of the surface and to flatten the world on it. While the western world seems to use the flat surface as a support to hold up a picture of a three dimensional world, the orientals recognize that the surface is two dimensional, leave it that way, and just beautify it. This is why each stroke means so much to them. Naturally, I can't paint that way because I'm not an oriental; my own style of painting can only be affected by my knowledge of the oriental's approach.

I think the theme of a portrait is as important as a likeness; a likeness dwells in an accurate drawing; the theme is housed in the handling of the medium. Use acrylics, or any medium for that matter, as a vehicle, or means, to materialize your concepts and ideas.

APPLYING MASS TONES

I didn't start this face with a shape of a shadow, as I usually do; I started with a flat mass tone of flesh for the entire face, a mass tone for the hair, and the same for the body and background. When that flesh area was dry, the shadow was put in with a wash of black and burnt umber. Then the flesh side was scumbled with a little lighter flesh tone to make the first flesh tone become the soft edges around the hair and the shadows.

FINISHING TOUCHES

The eyes, nose, and mouth were delineated with calligraphy, which is paint writing to me. It's a way to put in the final comments, a drawing over values. The hair and the blouse were painted in very dark gray. After they were dry, a wash of green and black was laid over the blouse, and the hair received a wash of darkened purple. I have no qualms about using black; I use it to assist the values of my color.

I wondered whether I should put highlights in the eyes. Even though I wanted a flat look, and wasn't using the five tone values that I usually rely on, I couldn't do without them. The highlights gave the eyes direction, and made them come alive.

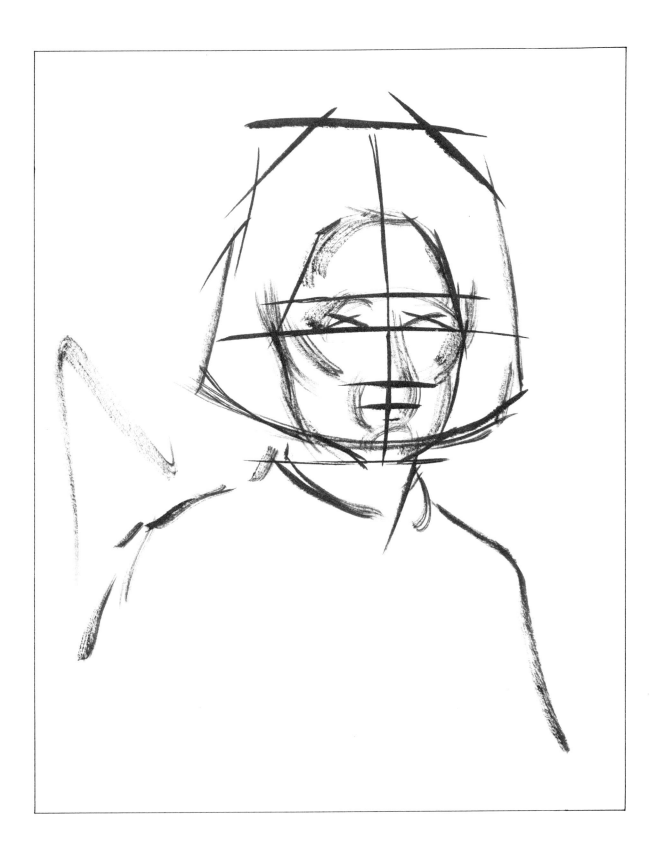

Step 1 I like to do the composition and drawing with a brush. Being a painter, I feel comfortable with a brush in my hand; it stops me from worrying about the looks of the lines I'm painting, so that I can just set down marks to indicate the proportion, perspective, and anatomy.

Step 2 Here are the elements of the composition painted in flat color mixed with water. The background: cadmium red light, red oxide, burnt umber, and a touch of white (all in admixture, of course); the hair and blouse: dark gray; the face: raw sienna, cadmium red light, and white. To give these areas depth, I glazed each one with color thinned with matte medium and water. A glazed area looks more luminous than a plain opaque application.

Step 3 I waited for the flesh area to dry, then with washes of burnt umber and black, I added the shadows to the face. Notice, though, that these shadows are treated in the same flat way I treated the rest of the picture. You've got to be consistent throughout; you can't change your direction once you've started without starting all over again. I also painted the shape of the hair and body out over the background.

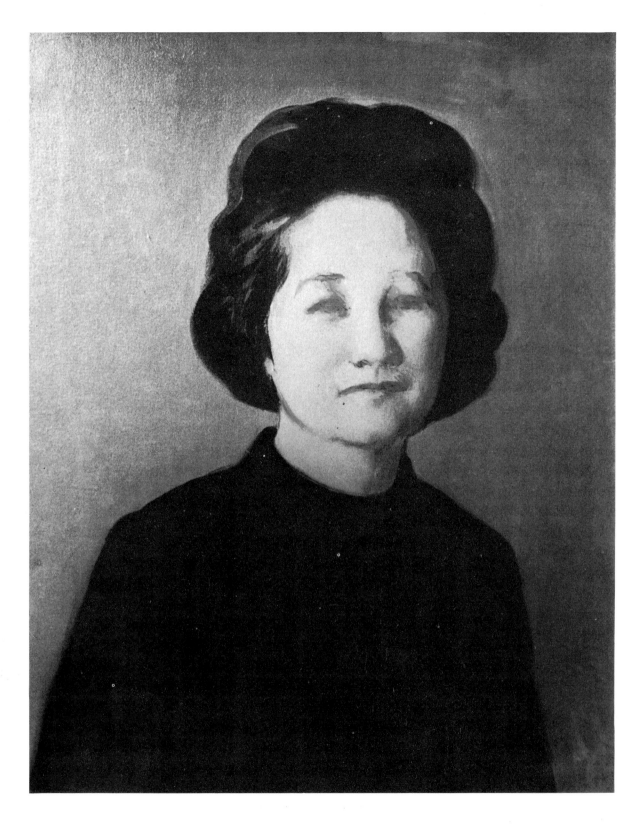

Step 4 (Above) The light planes of the face were lightened with a scumble of lighter flesh color. Scumbling with acrylics is a little easier to do if you add quite a bit of modeling paste to your mixture to make it semi-opaque.

Step 5 (Right) Here I placed the final touches of calligraphy, which I refer to as paint writing. I used a small red sable round brush, instead of the red sable script brush I usually use, because I wanted more control to record the correct shapes of the darkest darks. A wash of green and black was laid over the very dark gray blouse; darkened purple was washed over the hair.

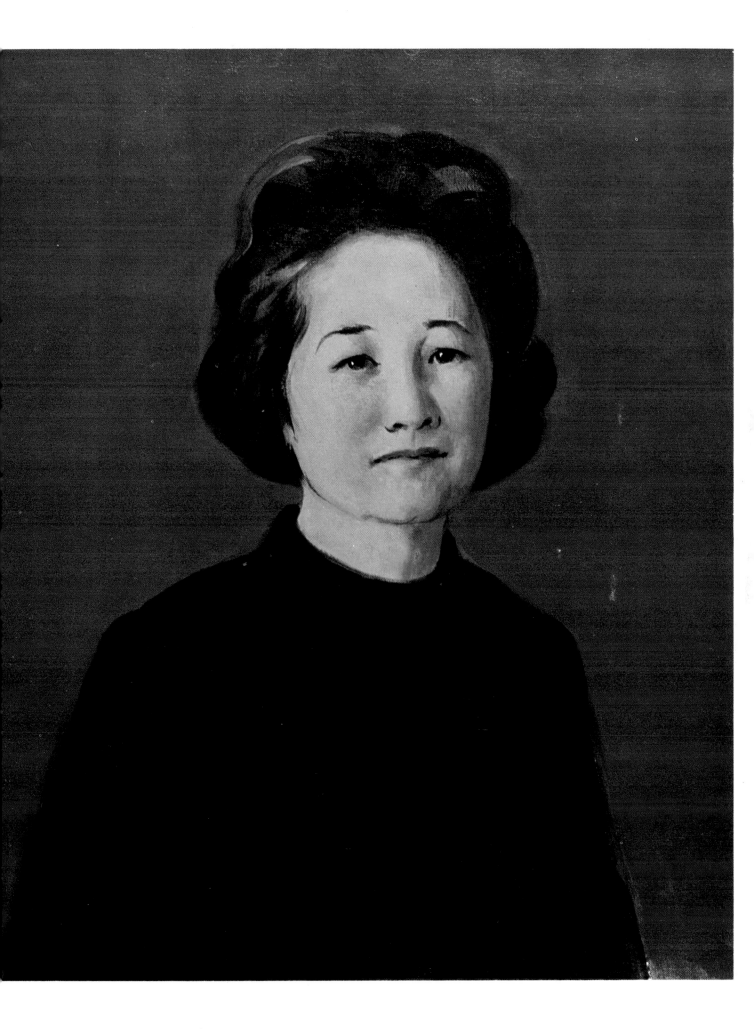

Demonstration 7 Using Watery Acrylics

Once I thought out a way to achieve a soft look with acrylics, I was able to approach this picture in a rather spontaneous manner. Acrylics have a reputation for being the "hard edge" paint, but I really feel that the quality of a picture isn't built in the paint as much as it is in the hands of the painter.

It's quite difficult to capture children's expressions, especially a smile. Very often a portrait of a little boy (or girl) looking directly at you seems too posed; it doesn't show a spontaneous or fleeting expression. For this reason, I chose to have him look away from me; this was the view I caught of him as he turned to look at his mother.

This kind of portrait lasts well. The child is going to grow out of the likeness depicted on the canvas, but the painting will be forever a picture of little "boy-dom," as well as a portrait of him as he was at that age.

CAPTURING THE IMPRESSION

I found it necessary to do a soft painting of this child because he wasn't a terribly good sitter (very few children this age are). I kept it vague rather than defined. As soon as you paint everything in sharp focus, you are forced to be extremely accurate. By keeping every area soft, you can succeed with an impression, rather than fail with an inaccurate record.

To get this soft look, I had to work with watery acrylics. Since water retards the drying rate of this paint, I nearly soaked the canvas with water. I painted the shadow pattern in an opaque gray (black, white, and Thalo green, cut down with a bit of cadmium red light to take the harshness away from the green). This application ran into the wetness of the canvas, much like a wet-in-wet watercolor. While the gray was still wet—and I didn't really have to rush—I painted in the light side of the face, chiseling the shapes into the wet gray-green shadow. While the right side of that shadow area was still wet, I put in some light background, keeping that edge as soft as could be. The edge was much softer in the beginning stages than in the finished painting, because the wet canvas made all the shapes blur. Softness has to be part of the beginning stage; you can't make it hard and then say you'll soften it up later. If you do, you'll just end up losing all the shapes, rather than having a chance to develop your picture toward stronger contrast.

I felt that the treatment of the subject so far necessitated a background that would look as spontaneous as the child's expression and as casual as my treatment of his hair, face, and clothing. I wanted a light tone next to the shadow side and needed a dark tone against the light side of the image. The square pattern on the right was suggested by a canvas that was on an easel behind the model. I have to be impressed visually in order to come up with an idea. Although I don't have to set down what it really is, I take from nature or take from my view whatever patterns I think my pictures need.

Step 1 The size and placement of the boy on the canvas. I can't stress enough the importance of establishing a composition first. A common mistake is starting with the drawing rather than a simple placement. Composition contributes the most to the mood of the portrait.

Demonstration 7: Using Watery Acrylics 127

Step 2 This illustrates the soft beginning stage effected by painting into a wetted surface with paint greatly thinned with water. The shadow pattern was painted with a mixture of black, white, and Thalo green cut with a bit of cadmium red light. The light side was painted in while the gray mixture on the dark side was still wet. I chiseled the flesh colors into the shadow.

Step 3 The finished painting. More contrast was used to put the image into focus. It was softer in the beginning stages because of the extreme wetness of the surface which made the shapes blur. To achieve a soft look, you have to start soft; you can't begin hard with hopes of softening it at the end stages.

Demonstration 8 Painting the Beard Area

This type of individual is just perfect for the way I love to paint, and for the way I seem to paint naturally: broadly and with very little adornment. Luke's a farmer and has a good, direct look. His endorsing expression and his facial appearance reminded me of my uncle, who was also a farmer. Maybe this is why I felt a kinship with Luke. As he posed for me, he said he didn't feel self-conscious at all, even though his life on the farm was so foreign to the studio of a portrait painter. He felt at ease because I mentally made him my uncle.

ESTABLISHING THE BEARD

Many people have asked me who's easier to paint, men or women. Technically, they're equally difficult—the smooth, lovely quality of a woman's skin is just as hard to record as trying to get the feeling of the growth of a beard. The coloration and value of a beard should not dirty the light portion of the face and make it recede. This color still has to lay on the same plane as the areas of skin not shadowed by the growth of hair. The color you see on the upper lip and from the ears down onto the chin should be a warm color, even though it's relatively cool compared to the upper part of the face. If it's a cool color, it's liable to look like a five o'clock shadow and push the chin back, rather than have it project.

I painted the beard area by using greatly reduced warm color. For instance, in my flesh mixture, I added burnt umber and, oddly enough, cadmium yellow light. These two yellows (the light, bright one and the darker, less intense one) combined to make a gray. I added more white to this mixture of dulled flesh so that the burnt umber didn't darken the flesh value.

Another way to "grow" a beard with acrylics is to ignore the color of the beard entirely as you paint in the flesh area. When the flesh area is dry, glaze the bearded area with gel and a little raw umber.

Working on a small canvas didn't deter me from wanting to paint the head life size; in fact, I wanted it even *larger* than life. Ordinarily, the chin shouldn't fall much lower than the center of the canvas from the top down, but this only applies to canvases over 18" x 22". On a smaller canvas, you can't place the chin halfway down the middle because you'll miniaturize the face so much that a realistic concept will be lost.

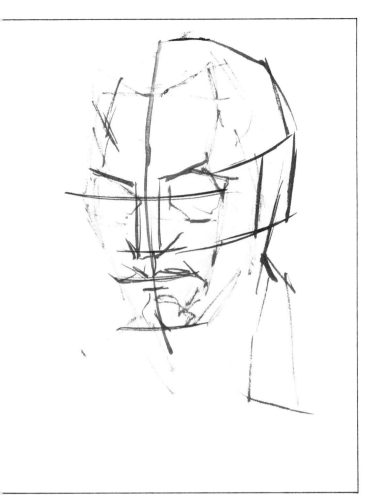

Step 1 The composition and drawing, life size on a small canvas. Mentally draw an X through the center of the canvas. You'll see that Luke's chin is well below the cross. Only on canvases smaller than 18″ x 22″ can you disregard the rule of keeping the chin above the exact center of the canvas.

Step 2 The light area was painted in tones to represent the darker flesh colors on the illuminated planes after the shadows on the face, background, and body were painted in very dark gray. The color you see on the areas where the beard grows should be put in with a warm color, despite its relative coolness to the upper part of the face.

Step 3 (Above) The flesh area was painted again, leaving the original flesh color to serve as a blender into shadow. After mixing my color, I wiped much of the paint off my brush with my rag. With this smaller amount of paint on my brush, I eased the color on with my strokes. I added the glasses over the dried flesh area. (No matter what medium you use, always paint the glasses over dry or almost dry color. Another point about glasses: don't paint a portrait of them; the simpler they're done the better.) I find that with acrylics I work the light area up separately from the rest of the picture's development. I can put slightly different tones side by side, and they seem to blend to make the many nuances of shapes in the face.

Step 4 (Right) To finish the picture, I painted the background and added the darkest tones. Another way to paint the beard is to disregard it and then, when dry, glaze the bearded area with a little raw umber mixed with gel. This is easy to do with fast-drying acrylics.

Demonstration 9 A Quick, Direct Approach

This boy seemed very direct. As he sat, he found it embarrassing to look at me, so he took it upon himself to turn and look away. He then posed very quietly in this position, without much enthusiasm, but with a great deal of cooperation. He must have been thinking, "Well, I have to pose, and my mother told me to sit still, so I'll sit still." Looking at him, I saw that he was living in his own world and, as I painted, this is what seemed to come forth on my canvas.

We don't really try for an effect, we just get one. And we can only get an effect if we form some kind of impression from our model. This is what makes painting an automatic self-expression, and this is what makes a portrait painter. I contemplate the way people are; this *has* to affect me. This is what tempts me to paint them, and I hope these thoughts become a pictorial record of my impressions.

THE TECHNIQUE

My approach to this painting was very direct. I never really thought about the paint; I just started and reacted to the needs of the painting as it progressed. Except for the background, I used one brush: a #18 red sable bright. This big brush enabled me to work the planes of the face rather broadly.

This picture was done without modeling paste, gel, or retarder, just paint thinned with water, and not much water at that. I picked up big gobs of paint with my brush to insure a good coverage in one application. The painting is all just one layer of paint. This technique, called wet-into-wet, means that you do a layer and then work into that wet layer. I think it should be called wet-*on*-wet. But since one entire layer has to be put down first before you can paint over it, wet-*on*-wet can't be done with acrylics. You can, however, paint wet *next* to wet with this fast-drying paint. For example, in this portrait, the forehead was completed and then the portions next to the forehead were painted while the paint was still wet.

After placing and proportioning the head, I put in the whole front plane of the face in gray and then chiseled in the light left side of the face into the shadow. The gray that I used for the shadow wasn't as cool as I usually start with; it was a warm gray made of burnt umber, white, Thalo blue, and a bit of cadmium yellow. That original mixture is still the shadow side; the eyes, nose, and mouth were put in with darker local color.

I like to work in this manner, but it *has* to turn out right. The only thing to do if it doesn't is to start over again.

Step 1 I often find it easier to chop in a drawing with a series of straight lines. By limiting myself this way, I'm forced to make many observations. My model seemed embarrassed whenever he looked at me. I noticed he was more at ease when he looked away, so I painted him in that attitude. Once comfortably situated, he cooperated beautifully.

Step 2 The pattern of the shadow was painted larger than it really was so the light shape could be cut into it. This is hard to get some beginners to do, because they're afraid that their light tones may be darkened or muddied by the darker shadow tones. I find many of them coloring in a drawing rather than painting a painting. This approach makes them paint a tone right up to an edge they've either actually drawn in or one that they've fixed in their minds.

Step 3 This is the beginning of the lay-in of flesh color around the eye, which, along with the nose and mouth, was put in with darker local color. This was placed on top of the original mixture, which is still the shadow side.

Demonstration 9: A Quick, Direct Approach   137

Step 4 (Above) Finished, except for the darker darks. Working this way, I like to start with medium lights and medium darks. This gives me great leeway to go lighter and lighter until I'm close to pure white, which I won't use, and darker and darker until I'm close to pure black, which I won't use either.

Step 5 (Right) This technique of painting is called *alla prima*, which means all at once. Working this way, you're painting tone and color at the same time. It's popularly referred to as *wet-into-wet*, but I think it should be called *wet-on-wet* because you're working *onto* a wet layer instead of into it. No matter what it's called, this technique requires years of experience to be done correctly. There's no shortcut to this kind of handling. Experience is something that can't be learned or taught.

Demonstration 10 A More Formal Portrait

This gentleman is the director of a hospital and school for crippled children. Despite his august position in the field of education and rehabilitation, he was far from the pompous individual that's popularly associated with that profession. In fact, John was a "regular Joe." All of these qualities had to be included in my portrait of him, determining for me that it would be rather formal. At the same time, though, I didn't want to lose any of his human quality, for he had a marvelous wit and great empathy for people. I had to try to choose a view of the model that best represented him. This is why he was so surprised when, after he struck a pose, I said, "No, that doesn't look like you."

"How can you know?" he asked. " You've just met me."

The view of him that I saw *didn't* look like him, even though I *had* just met him. This happens in photography too. How many times have you heard, "The camera never lies," and yet many photographs don't resemble their subjects. Don't always blame the camera; it's the man *behind* the camera who has to function in the same way as the painter behind the easel. He must size up his subject, and then choose the view that best says, "It *is* him."

FIRST SITTING

This picture was approached in this fashion. The head was done in one sitting, very fast; I'd say about an hour. I find that when I work with the model for a short period of time, I don't confuse the expression I want with second thoughts. I see something, and use my paints really fast to set it down. Naturally, this—or any—kind of approach needs correction later with a more critical eye. I can only get something right after I've set it down wrong. I don't purposely do it wrong, but my brush doesn't have a built-in guarantee of accuracy.

SECOND SITTING

The second sitting was used expressly to make the whole attitude of the face more plausible. There were certain hard edges and other areas that had been defined incorrectly; the glow of the highlight pattern from forehead to chin wasn't skin-like. It was a likeness of the man; it had everything except the likeness of the skin texture.

To begin my corrections, I put a layer of acrylic retarder over the entire face so that I could work into this with the little changes of value and color. It helped to adjust them as I laid them on top of the painting. This retarder gives a transparent effect, too, so these corrections or comments didn't ruin what I already had.

The comments I added into the shadow were done with quite a bit of water. I could call them glazes, but I think of the word glaze more in terms of oil applications. Acrylic is an aqueous medium, and so I feel that a transparent application in acrylics should be called a wash. I paint in a dark area, then clean my brush, and with a little clean water, I blend it out much the way a watercolorist works a graded wash.

Step 1 My usual bold start. You can't be timid. Once you've made up your mind about what has to be done, move your paint into action. Painting isn't difficult; the thinking and deciding is. Since this was to be done in one sitting, I was able to set down an instantaneous impression without any fear of second thoughts interfering with the attitude. I found out later, though, that another sitting would be necessary.

Step 2 At the end of the first sitting, I discovered that one eye was higher than the other. Compare this step with the finished painting, you'll notice this in the left eye— as you view the picture. These things do happen. Fortunately, the model was available for an additional sitting, even though he was told initially there'd be only one. These are the things you can't forecast, and because you can't you've got to have escape hatches such as both you and your model being available for the necessary corrections.

Step 3 (Above) I find that correcting with acrylics is easy. I removed the error by remassing the area in colored tones common to that area's surroundings: dark if the mistake's in shadow; light if it's on the light side. I had to get rid of the wrong shape before I could repaint a more correct one. Now you can see that the face is less finished than it was in Step 2. This offered me a chance to develop the painting further by adding the subtle applications of lighter lights and darker darks.

Step 4 (Right) To finish the picture I had to get it back to the stage it was in before I had started to correct the eye. You just can't correct an area without affecting everything around it. The added, final comments into the shadow were done with washes of color. Getting that finished look can be compared to putting on the final coat of varnish on a piece of furniture. First you must build the painting, then you have to sand down its harshness so that the final application can refine the painting.

Demonstration 11 Relating the Head to a White Background

What a pretty age to be painted! This model motivated me to handle my paint with more care than I usually do right from the beginning. I also wanted a white background which always puts me in a more careful mood. Using a white background causes a different color attitude toward skin. You have to work in a lighter key or else the head will look like a dark blot against the white. And using a white background makes the skin cooler.

The whites of the eyes were painted with a cool gray-blue, in keeping with the cooler flesh. The value of this cooler gray-blue is much the same value as that of the flesh. A mistake many people make in painting eyes is to make the whites of the eyes too light.

I mixed large amounts of gel into my lighter cooler additions to the flesh area. Gel makes the application of even an opaque mixture transparent, thus adding a subtle comment, rather than a strong statement, to what has already been painted.

These cooler additions onto the basic flesh area were pink mixtures: white and cadmium red light or white and red oxide. Reddish flesh tones are cool compared to orange ones. Remember, color is a very relative condition.

Step 1 I wanted to paint this charming young lady against a white background. As soon as that decision was made, I had to direct my entire procedure to it. A minimum amount of lines were used to place the head, and a very thin wash of gray located the effect of the lighting. In order to keep this picture in a high key, I had to start that way.

Step 2 Using a white background makes the skin cooler, so I had to gear everything to it. When using a white background, you must work in a lighter key or the head will look like a dark blot. I set down a very light-toned shadow pattern (black, blue, and white) with little contrast to the flesh color. Then, I began the hair in a grayed burnt sienna.

Step 3 (Above) The shadow was darkened and more defined. The hair was made darker and its shape was painted more accurately. In keeping with the cooler flesh, the whites of the eyes were painted with a cool gray-blue. Many beginners mistakenly paint the whites of the eyes pure white. Their portraits end up looking as though the models had electric light bulbs inside their heads.

Step 4 (Right) To finish the picture, I mixed large amounts of gel into cooler mixtures of flesh. I used white, cadmium red light, and red oxide; reddish flesh tones are cool compared to orange ones. I glazed this over my basic flesh tone.

Demonstration 12 Utilizing the Versatility of Acrylics

Dave's mother was a Sioux Indian, and his father was Welsh. I met him in Sioux Falls, South Dakota, and thought he was very nice. I asked him to pose for me, because I was intrigued with his face and complexion. I also thought his portrait would be an interesting addition to this book.

TEXTURE AND BACKGROUND

The skin color of the American Indian is definitely red. It's not swarthy or olive like that of the people of the Mediterranean; and it's not yellow like that of the oriental. Dave's skin was smooth and beardless.

I used strong reflected light to record the shine caused by these characteristics. Often smoothness is easier to show in shadow. You see this when painting porcelain and other shiny surfaces. I'd like to stress the importance of painting still life before you paint portraits. Still life subject matter gives you a chance to observe and represent textural effects. The texture of Dave's hair was different from that of other hair I'd painted. Making skin look like skin and hair like hair is an essential part of a complete likeness and a good portrait. It's also important to approach a portrait with freedom. You can't worry about the craft of painting while you're concentrating on recording a personality. Freedom comes from confidence, which is gained from experience.

I didn't want to lose the way Dave looked, so as quickly and as simply as possible, I tried to set down the position of the face. I used a pose that suggested the inscrutable Indian. I put the background in a flat mass tone. I was going to leave it that way, but later decided that it needed something, so I painted in colors, using a rhythm of application that represented an Indian rug. Furthermore, I felt a little more texture in the background would prove more interesting. How can I say why I do these things? They're all a matter of a thought that results from what I think the picture needs. The background describes the Indian side of Dave. When painting, costuming isn't a matter of clothing; it's costuming the canvas to make a presentation that counts.

Step 1 To present the composition, I made an application of color that covered the canvas well. Acrylics cover better in one application than oil colors do. I seldom use a wash as a beginning stage. I like to work *on* to paint rather than to repaint. When these values were dry, I glazed red oxide over the entire face, Thalo blue on the hair. I used water to thin my paint for these glazes, because I didn't want my painting to shine, which gel and the other mediums would have made it do.

Step 2 Here I developed the background in tones of yellow ochre, and, as always, I intentionally wrecked the outline. I worked lighter tones into the flesh area, using color thickened with modeling paste. This retarded the drying, which gave me time to work. When this was dry, I glazed again, this time with burnt sienna. Glazes darken an area and this gave me a chance to build up with lighter lights again, this time with no modeling paste added to the color.

Step 3 (Above) By this time, I had built up the lights as light as I wanted them. I dragged small amounts of color over color with the flat of a broad red sable brush to soften some areas. I refined the background and glazed some colors here and there. I redid the hair, and lightened the inside of the shadow with a scumble, leaving the turning edge dark. I carefully added some washes of dark to the eyes, nose, and mouth.

Step 4 (Right) The finished picture. I put a layer of retarder over the face, and added the reflections, highlights, and any subtle tones that I felt would improve the expressional likeness. Newcomers to acrylics have asked me how their drying time could be retarded. I generally tell them to paint with oils if they want a slower drying medium. However, there are times that you prefer to have your acrylic application stay wet, just as I wanted in this stage.

Demonstration 13   Blending Hair and Edges

I was initially intrigued by Anita's long dark hair and piercing black eyes that were contrasted by her soft pink dress. As the picture progressed, other qualities began to come out: Anita was a beautiful woman, and it was only under close scrutiny that her beauty became so evident.

Painting Anita served a dual purpose. The first one is obvious—I *wanted* to paint her. In the second place, the picture would give me the chance to show you how to blend hair and edges. Too many students paint portraits that seem as though the heads were cut out and pasted onto the backgrounds.

Step 1 After putting down a line for the top of the head and one for the chin, I dragged some dark tones over the tooth of the canvas to plan my picture.

Step 2 Then I painted the flesh side of the face, a shadow side, a background, and hair area. These mass tones, done rather roughly, got rid of the white canvas. I could then direct all my attention to the turning point, or the edge where the flesh color darkens into shadow. You'll notice a medium tone between the body tone and body shadow. This was put in over an existing edge that was too sharp. This medium tone of white, black, yellow ochre, and cadmium red light, mixed with acrylic retarder, made it possible to repaint the flesh color into it on one side, and the shadow tone into it on the other.

Step 3 (Above) The turning edge was softened by the progress of the previous step, and the darker darks added into the shadow. Now the background was repainted in a light gray-green, the clothing in pink. These two colors were blended together where they met. The background tone and hair tone were blended together, and the hair shape was made smaller than it really was, so that I could let my subsequent brushstrokes of hair color feather out over the background to make the image stand in front of it. The flesh color was painted beyond the hairline so I could comb the hair color over the flesh tone. I started my stroke in the hair area, and pulled the brush away as I neared the hair line.

Step 4 (Right) The finished picture. I added the usual lighter tones to the flesh and I highlighted the hair. The portrait's color mood improved when I glazed the background and clothing with a mixture of Thalo crimson and cadmium red light, greatly thinned with water.

Taking Advantage of a Toned Canvas

This is a portrait of a very studious young man, who is majoring in geology. He's not typical of the young American college boy. He had been in the army for six years, and served in Vietnam with the Green Berets. His contemplative nature seemed to be recorded by his habit of biting his glasses. He wears them all the time, but when he took them off and bit on them, I thought this attitude looked most like him. As I've said before, you have to get a view of the model that seems to represent him rather than just be a picture of him. I couldn't see painting Henry the way I had painted Luke. No, Henry is too mysterious and complex to be painted directly. His complexity of personality motivated a more profound use of the material. You see, a portrait painter can't see in terms of skin, hair, eyes, nose, and mouth; he has to see people as paint and then turn the paint into an interpretation of the model.

Step 1 This painting was done on a canvas toned somewhat unevenly with a big brush, using raw sienna, red oxide, and Mars violet in admixture. When it was dry, I sketched Henry in with white chalk. The main thing I wanted to maintain was the tone of the canvas affecting the entire image, except where the light was striking very directly. The white chalk was used to make corrections without ruining the tone of the canvas.

Demonstration 14: Taking Advantage of a Toned Canvas 157

Step 2 After the lines for the top of the head, the chin, the eyes, the nose, and the pose were placed, the illuminated planes were painted in with a value not as light as you see in the finished picture. This mixture was cadmium red light, yellow ochre, burnt umber, and white. A touch of Mars violet was added to make it look much like the canvas color, only lighter. I did this to effect a blend into shadow.

Step 3 As the light side was put in, the tone of the canvas acted as the shadow tone, and as I reached the shadow portion of the face, I wiped off much of my paint from my brush, and dragged it over the tooth of the canvas. Then the light area was built up lighter. And each time it was built up lighter, the lighter tone was dragged into the tone that was already there. It was completely painted in layers of wet paint dragged onto dry paint.

Step 4 The shadow of the face was then put in with a
wash of burnt umber, and then the darker dark accents
of eyelashes, eyes, underplanes of the nose, mouth, and
underplanes of the chin were put in with a cooler version
of burnt umber (a touch of blue was used to tone down
the umber).

Step 5 The shirt was done with black and white, greatly thinned with water so that it just washed over the toned canvas. Then that mixture was made a little thicker—meaning that I used less water—and added where you see the tone getting a little lighter; and then almost with no water where the light strongly struck the top of the shirt. This tone was dragged on so it fused in softly. The background color served as the unity of the composition, and kept the picture calm.

Demonstration 15   The Self-Portrait

The self-portrait is the easiest portrait to paint. My concentration isn't affected by a sitter, and I have the most patient and cooperative model in the world. I never have to wait for the right pose, and when I get tired of painting, my model rests with me. We even share the same cup of coffee.

I think that painting a self-portrait exposes your true style of painting, because you're not affected by anyone. It's doing a portrait for sheer study; it's art for art's sake. I can't help but think of Rembrandt whenever I paint myself. His many self-portraits make me think of him more personally than other painters of the past. They also make me feel as though we have something in common other than both being Dutch. No, I wouldn't dare compare myself with Rembrandt as a painter, but I'm sure he must have been left-handed, just as I am. Many of his self-portraits show him in a pose that I see of myself in the mirror as I paint. I, too, have done many self-portraits; the ones done in art schoool bit the dust, but I feel they gave me hours of valuable study. I still have one I did nine years ago, and the one in this book looks even younger. That's another thing you can take advantage of when you paint yourself.

Many students have asked me how I can pose and paint at the same time. This question always gives me an excellent chance to explain that I look at an area, and mix the color and tone of that area. With this mixture ready on my brush, I relook to see the shape of the area, and then translate it into brushstrokes.

The study of painting is learning how to see, and knowing what to look for.

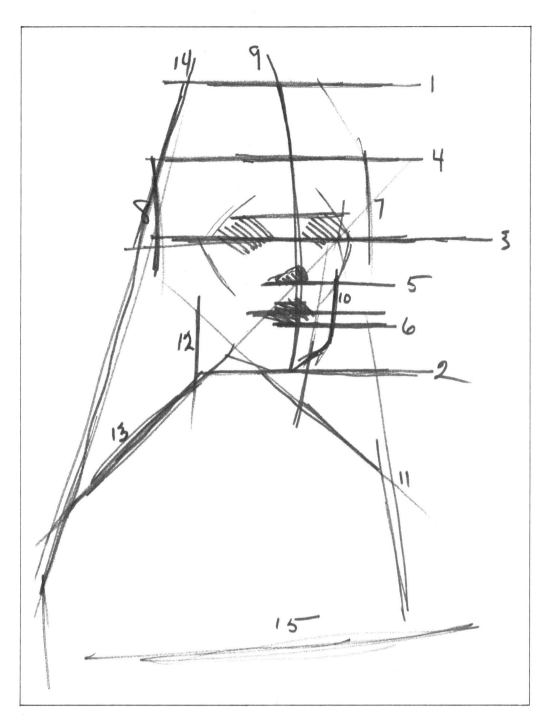

Step 1 This chart shows how I placed the head and how I measured the basic proportions for my self-portrait. Line 1 indicates how far down from the top of the canvas I wanted the head to be. Then, to determine its size, I actually measured my head. The chin line became line 2. Now that I had my over-all size, I was able to divide it into fractions as follows: Line 3 is where the eyes were located; this is the space between the top of the head and the chin—little more than one half the entire shape. Line 4 locates the hairline, halfway between the eyes and the top of the head. Line 5 is one third of the eyes to the chin area; that's where I planned the nose to be. Line 6 is also one third of the eyes to the chin area (the lower third); that's where the lower lip was placed. Now I had to determine the width. I measured my head and found its width equal to the distance from hairline to chin. These outside dimensions were located with lines 7 and 8, only after I decided where I wanted the head to be placed from side to side on the canvas. Line 9 was then put in; this was dictated by my pose, how much of a three-quarter view I wanted. These proportions then told me how much width there would be on the right side of the face (actually it's my left cheek), and I set that down as line 10. The remainder of my proportioning was determined by what I call "angling." I hold my brush along a line of the image, observing where my brush intersects other shapes already placed. I start my line from that intersection, and make my stroke follow my brush handle. These maneuvers are indicated by lines 11, 12, 13, and 14. Finally, I measured from the chin area to the middle of the breast, and, finding it equal to the head size, I set the mark down (line 15). Now I was ready to paint.

Step 2 The lines in Step 1 became a guide for my dark tones representing the shadow pattern in gray. While filling in the light area with a light gray, I corrected that pattern. All of my cartography, naturally, was covered by the opaque gray applications, which points out that you shouldn't be timid about your preliminary construction lines. Put them in strongly; they serve as the security.

Step 3 I decided on a dark gray-green background, and as I painted it in I corrected the shape of the hairdo. I then concentrated more carefully on the exact shape of the shadow that fell on the features of the face. With flesh tone for the lights and gray for the shadow, I started from the top down. Notice the forehead, eye area, cheeks, and nose are now better shapes.

Step 4 (Above) I modeled lighter tones into the light area of the face. The subtle nuances of slightly darker value on the flesh are actually the flesh tones of Step 3. I darkened the hair color, and put in the body, palette, and brushes in a reduced tone.

Step 5 (Right) The finished self-portrait. I added lighter tones to show the hairdo, and darker tones to show the details of the eyes, nose, and mouth. Reflected light was painted into the shadow. All the finishing up additions to the face were done with my acrylic colors greatly thinned with water so the tones could flow over what I had already done. My blouse was many colors.

Self-portrait by M. A. Rasko, the subject of a copy that now hangs in my studio as a constant reminder of what he means to me.

Demonstration 16   How to Work From a Photograph

I've included this chapter on copying because I know that anyone who paints, either as a hobby or professionally, is asked to work, or copy, from a photograph. In my twenty years of painting portraits professionally, I've done quite a few copies. Anyone who wanted to commission me to do a copy had to be armed with two things: very good reference material, and a very convincing story of why the picture should be painted. Even though copying isn't the creative adventure that working from life is, I enjoy the challenge it imposes on my craftsmanship.

One that intrigued me was a primitive painting that one sister owned and another sister wanted. My copy of it restored the peace, much to the relief of their family, and as I painted the portrait I gained more respect for primitives with their seemingly flat faces.

Then there was the couple who commissioned me to copy portraits of ancestors that were painted by John Wesley Jarvis, a fine, little known, early American painter. They were beautiful portraits, much like those of Gilbert Stuart. To emulate the technique of the past, I used acrylic for the underpainting, glazing color on in oil.

I even was commissioned to copy one of my own portraits of a mother of sixteen children. When she died, I was asked to make a copy of it. I'm glad I wasn't commissioned to do sixteen; the spark and spontaneity of the original was hard to repeat.

Of all the copy assignments I've done, none was more pleasant than the one of combining a painting with a photograph. The subject was a little girl, the painting was Joshua Reynolds' *The Age of Innocence*. It was commissioned by a woman—the child's great aunt—who had seen seven girls in her family grow up to young womanhood before she could have their portraits done in the attitude of Reynolds' painting—her very favorite picture. She wasn't going to let her great niece's age pass her by. I agreed to do the painting, and she supplied me with a print of the painting and a spendid photograph in somewhat the same pose. The painting I did from this reference material is pictured in this chapter. I employed the method of acrylic underpainting in this one too.

SQUARING OFF

The most difficult part of copying is making it absolutely accurate to the original, which can only be done mechanically without getting a stiff, mechanical look. I square off the original and my canvas to insure accuracy, as many artists do, but I have a little trick that permits me to copy with the same technique you've just seen in my step-by-step demonstrations.

After I make the squares the size I need them on my canvas, I make the same squares on a piece of acetate that's the same size as my canvas. After transferring the drawing from the photo to the canvas by following each square, I begin to

 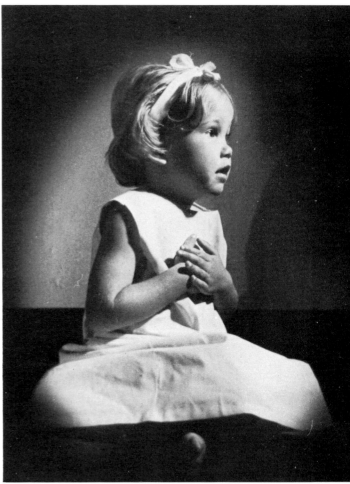

The Age of Innocence by Joshua Reynolds. This was one of the elements for the composite copy I was commissioned to paint.

A photograph of the subject posed in the same attitude as Reynolds' painting.

The finished picture (right). Since the photograph was excellent, I only used the Reynolds painting to aid me with the background and general coloration. I was glad the child posed in contemporary dress, rather than in a replica of Reynolds' model. As you can see, this was insignificant; the re-creation of the attitude and background was enough to suggest *The Age of Innocence*. I even omitted the child's feet; leaving them in, I felt, would have looked awkward. The challenge of the composite, and being able to improvise the way I did, added up to make this copy one of my favorites.

paint. Since all of my squares are painted away in the initial mass tones, I lay the squared acetate over my painting as I progress to check with the original. My discipline is the squared acetate, which is the whole key to developing the copy freely.

I learned that freedom comes from discipline from Maximilian Aureal (he preferred just M. A.) Rasko. He was a task master as a teacher, stressing the law and order that nature imposes on the elements that a painter uses to put his pictures together. He taught basic principles until they came out of my ears. But I began to feel comfortable with them, and the more I did, the freer I felt in front of the easel. It was his discipline that injected some sense into my natural style of painting. When Rasko died in 1961, I copied his self-portrait. It hangs in my studio, keeping his memory alive, and constantly reminding me of those wonderful sessions of his discipline, criticism, and lectures. This book is dedicated to him; I thought you should know why.

Index

Edited by Susan E. Meyer
Designed by James Craig
Composed in ten point Electra by Atlantic Linotype Co., Inc.
Printed and bound by Toppan Printing Co., Ltd.